DAWN to DUSK
A TASTE OF HOLLAND

FROM THE HOLLAND JUNIOR WELFARE LEAGUE   HOLLAND, MICHIGAN

PUBLISHERS OF EET SMAKELIJK

CREDITS

Front Cover: Tulips: "Queen of Holland" and our renowned Tulip Time Festival each May. "Taken on a warm May morning after a light rain." —*Deborah Troutman*

Title Page: De Zwaan, authentic working Dutch Windmill at Windmill Island, Holland, Michigan. "Holland in the Springtime: windmills and tulips." —*Joel Spykerman*

Back Cover: A warm summer evening at dusk. —*Mark Tanis*

This cookbook is a collection of favorite recipes, which
are not necessarily original recipes.

Published by
Holland Junior Welfare League

Copyright© 1996 by
Holland Junior Welfare League
P.O. Box 1633
Holland, Michigan 49422

Library of Congress Catalog Number: 96-83765
ISBN: 0-9612710-0-0

Edited, Designed and Manufactured by
Favorite Recipes® Press
P.O. Box 305142
Nashville, Tennessee 37230
1-800-358-0560

Manufactured in the United States of America
First Printing: 1996   10,000 copies

To order "Eet Smakelijk" and "Dawn to Dusk," contact
Holland Junior Welfare League, P.O. Box 1633, Holland, Michigan 49422

$\mathscr{C}$ONTENTS

Holland—A City of Stories

Holland is a community full of stories and steeped in rich history, colorful people, and attractive sites. Nestled on the shore of Lake Michigan and the natural bay of Lake Macatawa, the city of Holland is one of our nation's treasures.

The first residents of this heavily forested area were Native Americans. The land between the Kalamazoo and Grand Rivers was the home of the Ottawas. The first "American" settlers who worked regularly with the Ottawas were Indian agent Isaac Fairbanks and missionary George N. Smith.

In 1846, Reverend Alburtus C. Van Raalte left the Netherlands to establish a new colony in the United States. A religious division with the state church in their homeland and tough economic times led the colonists on a trip that would culminate in a decision to pioneer on the shores of Black Lake (now Lake Macatawa). Van Raalte envisioned a new settlement cut out of virgin forest. He could never have imagined how successful the community he founded would become.

But that success did not come without trial. The first years were hard and the pioneers buried many of their friends and family. An orphanage was built but never occupied—local families took in children who lost their parents. Difficulties with the native residents forced the Indians to move north. But despite the hardships of these first years, the small band of Dutch settlers thrived. Twenty years after Van Raalte kneeled in the snow to bless this place, Holland featured two railroads, several hotels, and numerous churches.

A strong commitment to education led to the Pioneer school just a few years after the Dutch arrived. Hope College, a four-year liberal arts school that grew out of this pioneering effort, was chartered in 1866.

Tragedy struck again in 1871. On the same day as the Chicago fire, 80 percent of Holland burned to the ground. Fires swept down on various midwestern cities during that parched fall, making the disaster more acute. Remarkably, only one life was lost during the conflagration. Would the fledgling Dutch settlement survive this crisis?

Two individuals came to the fore to lead the community out of the ashes. Founder Van Raalte declared his intention to rebuild the city. Key to this effort was the decision of the leading employer, Isaac Cappon, to rebuild his tannery factory in Holland, Michigan. The home of this important industrialist is preserved as a museum on the corner of Ninth and Washington in Holland.

By the turn of the century Holland had become an industrial center. Firms specializing in furniture, shoes, sugar, and machine tools found Holland a favorable site to establish business. The Dutch had a strong work ethic and a sense of "covenant," which came from their Calvinistic roots.

During this same period (c. 1880–1930) a resort complex was developed at the harbor channel. Featuring two large hotels, an amusement park, attractive lake front cottages, beaches, and a nearby zoo, the areas known as Macatawa Park and Ottawa Beach became tourist destinations for people throughout the midwest who arrived by train and passenger ship. Other resorts, such as Castle Park just south of the Holland channel, were also popular destinations.

The proliferation of the automobile, several devastating fires, and the depression sealed the fate of these popular spots. The lighthouse, Big Red, is one of the few landmarks to survive from this interesting resort period.

For visitors, the focus returned to Holland as the Tulip Time festival was established in Holland in 1929. This annual event grew quickly and is now ranked as one of the top five festivals in attendance nationwide. To complement the festival and provide a showcase for the Dutch heritage, Windmill Island features an authentic Dutch windmill.

After the Second World War, Holland also became more culturally diverse. As the Dutch had one hundred years earlier, new immigrants came to settle in the community. Hispanics, Asians, and African Americans found work with Holland's farms and businesses and established their families here.

This important heritage and current cultural diversity have been a critical part of Holland's success. Van Raalte had a vision 150 years ago for a new community based on religious ideals, hard work, and a bright hope for the future. Holland still has each of these elements of strength and is a tribute to our founder's vision.

Larry J. Wagenaar, Associate Professor
Director, The Joint Archives of Holland

If you would like to know more about Holland's past, The Joint Archives of Holland is open for research Monday–Friday from 1:00 to 5:00 p.m. and mornings by appointment. The archives is located on the lower level of the Van Wylen Library at Tenth and College, on the campus of Hope College, Holland, Michigan.

Holland Junior Welfare League

The Holland Junior Welfare League, established in 1932, is a non-profit organization dedicated to enriching the lives of greater Holland area youth. This is accomplished through various service and fundraising projects run by our dedicated volunteers. The proceeds generated from *Dawn to Dusk* will be among the funds disbursed each spring to qualifying applicants that share in our passion for the welfare of our community's children.

All *Dawn to Dusk* recipes have been triple tested and have met our committee's stringent guidelines. The Holland Junior Welfare League is proud of this collection of elegant, yet easy, recipes and accompanying text and photographs. We hope you enjoy "A Taste of Holland."

A Note About Food and Wine

The most pleasurable way to enhance an elegant meal is to accompany it with well-chosen wine. When creating a menu, selecting wines to complement the meal may seem complicated and frustrating. However, by following these few simple guidelines, the process can be painless and even enjoyable.

- **The First Guideline:** Red wines should be paired with red meats while white wines are best paired with white meats. Though there are many exceptions, this principle is a good starting point for selecting wine.

- **The Second Guideline:** Pair similar characteristics of wine and food in order to enhance the traits they share. Stronger, hardier dishes are often well matched with "bigger" more intensely flavorful wines. A delicate dish is often best accompanied with a light and delicate wine.

  For example, a pork dish served with a rich cream sauce will likely pair well with a rich and creamy Californian Chardonnay. However, when grilled with garlic and pepper, the same pork is probably better suited with a light red such as a Pinot Noir or Spanish Rioja. A traditional marinara sauce served over pasta is easily paired with its regional counterpart, Italian Chianti, but other light reds, such as Californian Zinfandel, are just as suitable. Heavy beef dishes almost always go best with full-bodied reds like Cabernet Sauvignon and Merlot, as well as French Rhone-styled wines.

- **The Third Guideline:** When serving more than one wine during a meal, serve white before red and dry before sweet. When entertaining, begin the event with a dry sparkling wine or Brut Champagne. End the evening on a sweet note with a traditional Porto, a German Auslese, or a Late Harvest Riesling from Michigan.

- **The Final Guideline:** Choose wines that you enjoy. An excellent way to discover your own wine preferences as well as please many palates is to serve more than one wine with dinner. There is always something to be learned from every food and wine combination.

As contributed by:
Mr. Butch Ter Haar
Proprietor of Butch's Dry Dock
Holland, Michigan

$\mathscr{A}$CKNOWLEDGMENTS

The Holland Junior Welfare League extends our gratitude to the following organizations and businesses:

Holland Area Chamber of Commerce
Joint Archives of Holland
Photographic Concepts
Tulip Time Office
Holland Area Convention & Visitors Bureau
Holland Camera Club
Hope College
City of Holland/Soren Wolff
Steketee Van Huis, Inc./Roger Davis
Image Group/Mark Tanis
Butch's Dry Dock
Clearbrook Restaurant
Sandpiper Restaurant
Till Midnight Restaurant
The Alpen Rose Restaurant
Tom Nienhuis Catering
The Auburn Restaurant

$\mathscr{I}$f you would like to visit or to find out about Holland, Michigan, feel free to contact: Holland Area Chamber of Commerce, 272 East Eighth Street, Holland, Michigan 49423; Holland Area Convention & Visitors Bureau, 100 East Eighth Street, Holland, Michigan 49423; or Tulip Time Office, 171 Lincoln Avenue, Holland, Michigan 49423.

Breakfast In Bed

Big Red after an early snowfall;
another reason Michigan is truly a Winter Wonderland

View from Holland State Park on a February morning.

Breakfast in Bed

*Most requested recipe from **Eet Smakelijk**

Apple Coffee Cake

4 cups chopped apples

1/4 cup orange juice

1 1/2 teaspoons cinnamon

1/4 cup orange juice

1/4 cup milk

1/2 cup margarine, softened

1 cup sugar

4 eggs

2 1/2 teaspoons vanilla extract

3 cups flour

2 teaspoons baking powder

1/4 teaspoon salt

2 teaspoons brown sugar

Yield: 16 servings

- Mix the apples, 1/4 cup orange juice and cinnamon in a medium bowl.
- Combine 1/4 cup orange juice, milk, margarine, sugar, eggs, vanilla, flour, baking powder and salt in a large bowl; mix well.
- Layer the batter and apple mixture 1/2 at a time in a bundt pan sprayed with nonstick baking spray.
- Sprinkle with the brown sugar.
- Bake at 350 degrees for 1 hour and 10 minutes.
- Cool in the pan for 10 minutes.
- Remove to a wire rack to cool completely.
- Serve warm or cold.

Cinnamon Sour Cream Coffee Cake

3/4 cup finely chopped pecans

1 teaspoon cinnamon

2 tablespoons sugar

2 cups flour

1/2 teaspoon baking soda

1 1/2 teaspoons baking powder

1 cup butter, softened

1 1/2 cups sugar

2 eggs

1 cup sour cream

1 teaspoon vanilla extract

Yield: 16 servings

- Mix the pecans, cinnamon and 2 tablespoons sugar in a small bowl and set aside.
- Sift the flour, baking soda and baking powder together.
- Cream the butter, 1 1/2 cups sugar and eggs in a mixer bowl until light and fluffy.
- Blend in the sour cream.
- Add the flour mixture gradually, mixing well after each addition.
- Stir in the vanilla.
- Layer the batter and the pecan mixture 1/2 at a time in a buttered and floured 9-inch tube pan.
- Place the pan in a cold oven and set the temperature at 350 degrees.
- Bake for 55 minutes.
- *Note:* This coffee cake freezes well.

Dutch Coffee Cake*

1½ cups sifted flour

2 teaspoons baking powder

¾ teaspoon salt

¼ cup sugar

⅓ cup shortening

1 egg, beaten

⅓ cup milk

3 firm bananas, cut diagonally into ¼-inch slices

3 tablespoons butter, softened

⅓ cup sugar

⅓ cup flour

1 teaspoon cinnamon

½ cup chopped pecans

Yield: 8 servings

- Sift 1½ cups flour, baking powder, salt and ¼ cup sugar into a large bowl.
- Cut in the shortening until crumbly.
- Add a mixture of the egg and milk, stirring until a stiff dough forms.
- Spread the dough evenly in a greased 8x8-inch baking pan.
- Arrange the bananas over the dough, allowing the slices to overlap.
- Cream the butter in a mixer bowl until light and fluffy.
- Add ⅓ cup sugar and ⅓ cup flour gradually, beating well after each addition.
- Stir in the cinnamon and pecans.
- Sprinkle over the bananas.
- Bake at 375 degrees for 30 minutes; the coffee cake cannot be tested for doneness with conventional methods.
- Serve warm.

Nutty Pineapple Coffee Cake

1 (20-ounce) can crushed pineapple

1½ cups sugar

1 teaspoon baking soda

2 eggs

2 cups flour

½ teaspoon salt

½ cup packed brown sugar

¼ cup chopped pecans

¾ cup butter

½ cup sugar

1 cup evaporated milk

1 teaspoon vanilla extract

Yield: 15 servings

- Drain the pineapple, reserving half the juice.
- Mix 1½ cups sugar, baking soda, eggs, flour, salt, pineapple and reserved juice in a large bowl.
- Pour the batter into a greased 9x13-inch baking pan.
- Sprinkle with a mixture of the brown sugar and pecans.
- Bake at 350 degrees for 30 minutes.
- Mix the butter, ½ cup sugar, evaporated milk and vanilla in a saucepan.
- Cook until the mixture is hot and bubbly, stirring frequently.
- Pour the mixture over the coffee cake in the pan.

Overnight Coffee Cake

1 (16-ounce) package frozen dinner rolls
1 (4-ounce) package instant butterscotch pudding mix
1 cup packed brown sugar
2 tablespoons cinnamon
1/2 cup melted butter
1/2 cup chopped pecans

Yield: 16 servings

- Layer the dinner rolls, pudding mix, brown sugar, cinnamon, butter and pecans in the order given in a greased bundt pan.
- Cover the pan with foil and then a towel and let stand overnight.
- Bake, uncovered, at 350 degrees for 30 minutes.

Pecan Breakfast Bread

2 (8-count) cans crescent rolls

2 tablespoons butter or margarine

1/2 cup sugar

1 to 2 teaspoons cinnamon

1/4 cup chopped pecans

2 tablespoons honey

1/4 cup confectioners' sugar

2 tablespoons butter or margarine

1/2 teaspoon vanilla extract

1/3 cup pecan halves

Yield: 10 to 12 servings

- Separate the dough into triangles and spread with 2 tablespoons butter.
- Sprinkle with a mixture of sugar, cinnamon and chopped pecans.
- Roll up each triangle, starting at the wide end.
- Place rolls point sides down in a greased 5x9-inch loaf pan, forming 2 layers of 8 rolls each.
- Bake at 375 degrees for 35 to 40 minutes or until browned.
- Combine the honey, confectioners' sugar, 2 tablespoons butter and vanilla in a saucepan.
- Bring to a boil, stirring constantly.
- Stir in the pecan halves.
- Invert the baked bread onto a serving plate.
- Drizzle with the honey mixture.

RASPBERRY SWIRL COFFEE CAKE

¹/₄ cup butter, softened

¹/₃ cup sugar

1 egg

1 teaspoon vanilla extract

1 cup flour

2 teaspoons baking powder

¹/₈ teaspoon salt

¹/₃ cup milk

¹/₂ cup raspberry preserves

2 tablespoons butter

2 tablespoons sugar

¹/₂ teaspoon cinnamon

¹/₄ cup flour

Yield: 8 servings

- Cream ¹/₄ cup butter and ¹/₃ cup sugar in a mixer bowl until light and fluffy.
- Stir in the egg and vanilla.
- Add the 1 cup flour, baking powder, salt and milk; mix well.
- Pour the batter into a greased 8-inch round baking pan.
- Dot with the preserves.
- Cut through the preserves with a butter knife to form swirls.
- Mix 2 tablespoons butter, 2 tablespoons sugar, cinnamon and ¹/₄ cup flour in a bowl until crumbly. Sprinkle over the batter.
- Bake at 375 degrees for 25 to 35 minutes or until the coffee cake tests done.

Dutch Apple Bread*

2 cups flour
1 teaspoon baking soda
1 teaspoon salt
1 cup sugar
½ cup margarine, softened
2 eggs
2 tablespoons sour milk
1 teaspoon vanilla extract
2 cups finely chopped apples
2 tablespoons sugar
2 tablespoons flour
2 tablespoons butter
1 teaspoon cinnamon
¼ cup chopped pecans (optional)

Yield: 10 to 12 servings

- Sift the 2 cups flour, baking soda and salt together.
- Cream the 1 cup sugar and margarine in a mixer bowl until light and fluffy.
- Blend in the eggs and sour milk.
- Add the flour mixture gradually, mixing well after each addition.
- Stir in the vanilla and apples.
- Pour into a greased 5x9-inch loaf pan.
- Mix the 2 tablespoons sugar, 2 tablespoons flour, butter, cinnamon and pecans in a bowl until crumbly.
- Sprinkle over the batter.
- Bake at 350 degrees for 1 hour.
- Cool in the pan for 10 minutes.
- Remove to a wire rack to cool completely.

Applesauce Bread

This is wonderful on the day it is baked—and even better toasted on the days following.

2 eggs
2 cups applesauce
1 cup sugar
$\frac{1}{2}$ cup packed brown sugar
$\frac{1}{2}$ cup melted butter
4 cups flour
4 teaspoons baking powder
$1\frac{1}{2}$ teaspoons salt
1 teaspoon baking soda
2 teaspoons apple pie spice
$\frac{1}{2}$ cup raisins
$\frac{1}{2}$ cup chopped walnuts

Yield: 20 to 24 servings

- Mix the eggs, applesauce, sugar, brown sugar and melted butter in a bowl until smooth.
- Add the flour, baking powder, salt, baking soda and apple pie spice; mix well.
- Fold in the raisins and walnuts.
- Pour into 2 greased loaf pans.
- Bake at 350 degrees for 50 minutes to 1 hour or until the loaves test done.
- Cool for 1 hour before slicing.

CARROT BREAD

3 cups whole wheat flour

1/4 cup wheat germ

1 teaspoon salt

1 teaspoon baking soda

1 teaspoon baking powder

1 1/2 tablespoons cinnamon

3 eggs

1 1/2 cups canola oil

2 cups sugar

2 cups grated carrots

1 (4-ounce) can juice-pack crushed pineapple

2 teaspoons vanilla extract

1 cup chopped pecans

Yield: 20 to 24 servings

- Mix the flour, wheat germ, salt, baking soda, baking powder and cinnamon together.
- Beat the eggs, oil and sugar in a bowl.
- Stir in the carrots, pineapple, vanilla and pecans.
- Add the flour mixture gradually, mixing well after each addition.
- Pour into 2 greased loaf pans.
- Bake at 350 degrees for 45 minutes.

Cinnamon Raisin Bread

1½ cups flour

¼ cup sugar

1½ teaspoons salt

2 envelopes yeast

¾ cup milk

½ cup water

1 cup margarine

3 egg yolks

½ cup flour

¾ cup raisins

2½ cups flour

½ cup melted margarine

2 teaspoons cinnamon

½ cup sugar

Yield: 20 to 24 servings

- Combine the 1½ cups flour, ¼ cup sugar, salt and yeast in a mixer bowl.
- Combine the milk, water and 1 cup margarine in a microwave-safe bowl.
- Microwave on High for 3 minutes.
- Add the milk mixture to the flour mixture; beat at medium speed for 2 minutes.
- Add the egg yolks, ½ cup flour and raisins; beat at high speed for 2 minutes.
- Add enough of the 2½ cups flour to make a stiff batter, stirring with a wooden spoon.
- Chill, covered, for 2 hours.
- Divide the dough into 6 equal portions.
- Roll each portion into a long rope.
- Dip each rope into the melted margarine and then into a mixture of the cinnamon and ½ cup sugar.
- Braid 3 ropes together to form a loaf. Repeat the procedure with the remaining ropes.
- Place the loaves on baking sheets.
- Let rise in a warm place for 1 hour.
- Bake at 350 degrees for 20 minutes.

Dutch Harvest Bread*
(Vruchtenbrood)

2 cups flour

4 teaspoons baking powder

1/4 teaspoon salt

3/4 cup sugar

1/4 cup citron

1/4 cup currants

2 tablespoons chopped candied cherries

2 tablespoons chopped candied lemon peel

1/2 cup chopped pecans

2 eggs, beaten

1 cup milk

3 tablespoons melted shortening

Yield: 10 to 12 servings

- Sift the flour, baking powder, salt and sugar into a large bowl.
- Stir in the citron, currants, cherries, lemon peel and pecans.
- Combine the eggs, milk and shortening in a medium bowl.
- Add the milk mixture to the flour mixture, stirring just until the flour is moistened.
- Pour into a greased 5x9-inch loaf pan.
- Bake at 375 degrees for 1 hour.
- Cool in the pan for 10 minutes.

Poppy Seed Bread

3 cups flour

1½ teaspoons salt

1¼ teaspoons baking powder

2¼ cups sugar

3 eggs

¼ cup milk

1 cup plus 2 tablespoons vegetable oil

4 teaspoons poppy seeds

¼ teaspoon vanilla extract

1½ teaspoons almond extract

1¼ teaspoons butter flavoring

¾ cup confectioners' sugar

¼ cup orange juice

½ teaspoon almond extract

¼ teaspoon butter flavoring

½ teaspoon vanilla extract

Yield: 20 to 24 servings

- Mix the flour, salt, baking powder, sugar, eggs, milk, oil, poppy seeds, ¼ teaspoon vanilla, 1½ teaspoons almond extract and 1¼ teaspoons butter flavoring in a large bowl.
- Pour into 2 large or 4 small nonstick loaf pans.
- Bake at 350 degrees for 55 minutes.
- Mix the confectioners' sugar, orange juice and remaining flavorings in a bowl.
- Pour over the hot loaves.

CELESTIAL DOUGHNUTS

These doughnuts are "heavenly!"

2 envelopes active dry yeast

1/3 cup warm water

1/2 teaspoon sugar

1/3 cup melted vegetable shortening

1 1/2 cups milk, scalded, cooled
    to lukewarm

1/4 cup sugar

2 teaspoons salt

2 teaspoons vanilla extract

2 eggs

1/4 cup wheat germ

1/4 cup soy flour

1/4 cup oat bran

4 1/2 cups all-purpose flour

1 cup melted unsalted butter

2 cups sugar

2 teaspoons ground cinnamon

Yield: 36 servings

- Sprinkle the yeast over the warm water in a large mixer bowl and let stand for 5 minutes.
- Stir the yeast and 1/2 teaspoon sugar into the water.
- Set the mixture aside for 10 minutes or until foamy.
- Stir a mixture of the shortening and milk into the yeast mixture.
- Add the 1/4 cup sugar, salt, vanilla, eggs, wheat germ, soy flour, oat bran and 1 1/2 cups of the all-purpose flour; beat vigorously until blended.
- Stir in the remaining all-purpose flour and beat until smooth.
- Cover the bowl and let the dough rise in a warm place for 1 hour or until doubled in bulk; punch the dough down.
- Pat the dough 1/2 inch thick on a floured board.
- Cut the dough with a star cookie cutter.
- Place the doughnuts 2 inches apart on buttered baking sheets.
- Let the doughnuts rise for 20 to 30 minutes or until doubled in bulk.
- Bake at 400 degrees for 10 to 15 minutes or just until golden brown.
- Dip the doughnuts quickly into the melted butter; roll in a mixture of 2 cups sugar and cinnamon.

Dutch Apple Flappen*

Dutch Apple Flappen is a traditional holiday specialty.

6 large cooking apples
1 cup flour, sifted
2 teaspoons baking powder
1/4 teaspoon salt
1 tablespoon sugar
1 egg, beaten
1/2 cup milk
Shortening for deep-frying
Confectioners' sugar to taste

Yield: 12 to 18 servings

- Peel and core the apples. Cut into 1/3-inch round slices.
- Mix the flour, baking powder, salt and sugar in a large bowl.
- Combine the egg with the milk in a small bowl.
- Add the milk mixture to the flour mixture gradually; mix well for 2 to 3 minutes.
- Dip the apple slices into the batter.
- Deep-fry in hot shortening in a deep-fryer for 1 to 2 minutes or until golden brown.
- Sprinkle with confectioners' sugar.
- Serve warm or cold.

Nummy Christmas Breakfast Rolls

This recipe makes enough dough to prepare rolls three times.

2 envelopes yeast
½ cup lukewarm water
1½ cups milk
½ cup sugar
2 teaspoons salt
2 eggs, slightly beaten
½ cup shortening
7 to 7½ cups flour
6 tablespoons (about) butter, softened
6 tablespoons (about) brown sugar
½ cup (about) chopped walnuts
   or pecans
½ cup melted butter
½ cup packed brown sugar
½ cup chopped walnuts or pecans
1 tablespoon light corn syrup

Yield: 18 servings

- Dissolve the yeast in the lukewarm water.
- Combine the yeast mixture, milk, sugar, salt, eggs and shortening in a large bowl.
- Add 4 cups of the flour; beat well with a spoon.
- Add the remaining flour 1 cup at a time, keeping the dough as soft as possible.
- Knead the dough well and let rise; repeat the process for a finer-textured dough.
- Roll ⅓ of the dough ¼ inch thick into a 9x18-inch rectangle.
- Divide remaining dough into halves. Freeze dough for up to one month for later use.
- Spread the rectangle generously with the 6 tablespoons butter and 6 tablespoons brown sugar.
- Sprinkle with the ½ cup walnuts.
- Roll the dough up tightly, beginning at the wide side; pinch the edges to seal.
- Cut the roll into 1-inch slices.
- Place ½ cup butter, ½ cup brown sugar and ½ cup walnuts in a baking pan.
- Place the rolls slightly apart in the pan and let them rise.
- Bake at 350 degrees for 25 to 35 minutes or until browned.

LATE STARTS

THE TOURIST COTTAGES AT MACATAWA PARK

My thoughts changed to the days of yesterday.
I wondered about Frank Baum, the author of
"The Wizard Of Oz," and about the local
landmarks that influenced his writings.

Lois Lamb

LATE STARTS

*Most requested recipe
from **Eet Smakelijk**

Dutch Omelet

2 extra-large eggs
Salt to taste
Freshly ground pepper to taste
1 tablespoon snipped fresh chives
2 tablespoons butter
2 ounces Gouda cheese, sliced

Yield: 1 serving

- Whisk the eggs, salt, pepper and chives in a small bowl.
- Melt the butter in a 7-inch ovenproof skillet, swirling the butter to coat the skillet.
- Pour the egg mixture in the skillet when the butter begins to bubble.
- Place the cheese in the center of the egg mixture.
- Cook over low heat for a few seconds or until the egg mixture begins to set.
- Place the skillet in the oven under a preheated broiler.
- Broil just until the cheese melts.
- Remove from the oven.
- Fold the omelet in half carefully, using a spatula.
- Serve immediately.
- *Note:* May substitute finely chopped scallions for the chives.

Eggs Monterey

1½ cups cubed ham

8 ounces bacon, crisp-fried, crumbled

12 eggs

1 teaspoon seasoned salt

½ teaspoon pepper

1 (4-ounce) can green chiles

1½ cups shredded Monterey Jack cheese

1 avocado, thinly sliced

1 tomato, thinly sliced

Yield: 6 to 8 servings

- Spread the ham and bacon in the bottom of a greased 2-quart casserole.
- Beat the eggs, seasoned salt, pepper and chiles in a bowl.
- Pour over the ham and bacon.
- Bake at 325 degrees for 30 minutes or until set.
- Sprinkle the Monterey Jack cheese over the top of the baked layers.
- Arrange the avocado and tomato slices on top of the cheese.
- Place under the broiler and broil until the cheese is melted.

Pasta Frittata

An excellent brunch, luncheon or simple supper dish.

16 ounces spaghetti, cooked, drained

6 eggs

1/3 cup milk

2 cups shredded mozzarella or
   Monterey Jack cheese

2 medium tomatoes, chopped

1 medium cucumber, chopped

1 clove of garlic, chopped

1 tablespoon olive oil

Dash of vinegar

1/4 teaspoon salad herbs

Yield: 4 to 6 servings

- Press half the cooked spaghetti into a preheated skillet sprayed with nonstick cooking spray.
- Whisk the eggs and milk in a small bowl.
- Pour half of the egg mixture over the spaghetti in the skillet.
- Sprinkle with the mozzarella cheese.
- Press the remaining spaghetti over the cheese, spreading to cover.
- Pour the remaining egg mixture over the top.
- Cook over medium-high heat until the frittata is firm and golden brown on the bottom.
- Place a large plate face down over the frittata in the skillet.
- Invert the skillet, holding the plate over the top.
- Slide the frittata cooked side up back into the skillet.
- Cook until the frittata is firm and golden brown.
- Remove the frittata to a serving plate.
- Cut the frittata into wedges.
- Combine tomatoes, cucumber, garlic, olive oil, vinegar and salad herbs in a bowl; mix well. Spoon over cooled frittata.
- *Note:* May substitute warmed spaghetti sauce and Parmesan cheese for cold tomato dressing.

Feta and Spinach Scramble

½ cup frozen chopped spinach, thawed

12 eggs

½ cup milk

¼ teaspoon salt

¼ teaspoon pepper

Melted butter

1 cup shredded Monterey Jack cheese

½ cup crumbled feta cheese

½ cup finely chopped mushrooms

Yield: 8 to 10 servings

- Squeeze the excess water from the spinach.
- Beat the eggs, milk, salt and pepper in a bowl.
- Scramble the egg mixture in melted butter in a skillet until partially set.
- Fold in the spinach, Monterey Jack cheese, feta cheese and mushrooms.
- Cook until the cheese is melted, stirring constantly.
- Spoon into a serving dish.
- Serve hot.

Spinach Quiche

1 egg white, beaten

2 unbaked (9-inch) pie shells

1/2 envelope onion soup mix

3 tablespoons flour

2 (9-ounce) packages frozen creamed spinach, thawed

1 cup cubed ham

2 cups shredded Swiss cheese

1 egg

1 egg yolk

1/2 cup light cream

Yield: 12 servings

- Brush the egg white over the pie shells.
- Combine the soup mix, flour, spinach, ham and Swiss cheese in a bowl.
- Pour the spinach mixture into the prepared pie shells.
- Beat the egg, egg yolk and cream in a small bowl.
- Pour equal amounts of the egg mixture over the spinach mixture in each pie shell.
- Bake at 350 degrees for 45 minutes to 1 hour or until set.

Sausage and Egg Brunch Casserole

This make-ahead dish keeps you out of the kitchen as your guests arrive.

1½ pounds sausage
7 slices bread, cubed
12 ounces Cheddar cheese, shredded
4 eggs
½ teaspoon salt
2 cups milk
1 tablespoon Dijon mustard

Yield: 10 servings

- Brown the sausage in a skillet, stirring until crumbly and cooked through; drain.
- Arrange the bread cubes in the bottom of a 9x13-inch baking dish.
- Sprinkle the sausage and shredded Cheddar cheese over the bread.
- Beat the eggs in a mixer bowl.
- Add the salt, milk and mustard; mix well.
- Pour the egg mixture over the prepared layers.
- Chill in the refrigerator for 8 to 12 hours.
- Bake at 375 degrees for 30 to 40 minutes or until set.
- *Note:* May substitute cubed cooked ham for the sausage.

ZUCCHINI AND ITALIAN SAUSAGE QUICHE

1 unbaked (9-inch) pie shell
2 cups shredded zucchini
1/4 cup butter or margarine
5 sweet Italian sausage links
1 cup shredded Swiss cheese
4 eggs
1 cup milk
1/2 cup whipping cream
1/4 cup grated Parmesan cheese
1/2 teaspoon salt
1/4 teaspoon white or black pepper

Yield: 6 servings

- Bake the pie shell at 450 degrees for 8 to 10 minutes.
- Let stand until cool.
- Sauté the zucchini in 2 tablespoons of the butter in a large skillet for 5 minutes or until tender; drain.
- Remove the zucchini from the skillet; set aside.
- Remove the casings from the sausage links.
- Slice 1 sausage link into 1/2-inch thick rounds; set aside.
- Cook the remaining sausage in the remaining 2 table-spoons butter in the skillet, stirring until crumbly and cooked through; drain on paper towels.
- Spoon the zucchini into the pie shell.
- Sprinkle the crumbled sausage and Swiss cheese over the zucchini.
- Beat the eggs lightly in a large bowl.
- Add the milk, whipping cream, Parmesan cheese, salt and pepper; mix well.
- Pour the egg mixture over the prepared layers.
- Arrange the sausage rounds around the edge of the egg mixture, pressing down lightly.
- Bake at 450 degrees for 15 minutes. Reduce oven temperature to 350 degrees.
- Bake for 15 minutes longer or until the center of the quiche is set.
- Let stand for 3 to 5 minutes before serving.

Holiday Ham Wreath

This looks very festive on a holiday table.

1 cup frozen chopped broccoli
1/4 cup chopped parsley
2 tablespoons finely chopped onion
2 tablespoons mustard
1 tablespoon margarine, softened
1 tablespoon lemon juice
3/4 cup shredded Swiss cheese
8 ounces cooked ham or chicken, finely chopped
1 (8-ounce) can crescent rolls
1/4 cup grated Parmesan cheese

Yield: 6 to 8 servings

- Cook the broccoli using the package directions; drain.
- Combine the parsley, onion, mustard, margarine and lemon juice in a small bowl, stirring until smooth.
- Add the broccoli, Swiss cheese and ham, tossing lightly to mix.
- Separate the crescent rolls into 8 triangles.
- Arrange the triangles in a ring with the bases slightly overlapping and the points facing outward, leaving a 3-inch diameter circle open in the center on a greased baking sheet or baking stone.
- Spoon the ham mixture over the base of the triangles.
- Fold the points over the ham mixture, forming a wreath.
- Sprinkle with the Parmesan cheese.
- Bake at 350 degrees for 25 to 30 minutes.

Pigs in the Blankets*
(Saucijzenbroodjes)

This recipe is a Tulip Time tradition.

2³/₄ to 3 pounds sausage
3 cups flour
3 tablespoons baking powder
1 teaspoon salt
1 cup margarine
1 cup milk

Yield: 30 to 36 servings

- Shape the sausage by hand or with a fork into 30 to 36 portions.
- Sift the flour, baking powder and salt into a bowl.
- Cut in the margarine until crumbly.
- Stir in the milk.
- Shape the dough into a smooth ball.
- Roll ¹/₄ inch thick on a floured surface.
- Cut into strips about 3¹/₂ inches wide.
- Wrap each sausage portion loosely in a strip of dough.
- Place sausage rolls seam side down on an ungreased baking sheet.
- Pierce the top of each sausage roll with a fork.
- Bake at 400 degrees for 15 minutes.
- Reduce the oven temperature to 350 degrees.
- Bake for 15 minutes or until brown.
- *Note:* May freeze for up to 4 months.

Make-Ahead French Toast

½ cup melted butter

1 cup dark brown sugar

1 loaf French bread, sliced

6 eggs

1½ cups milk

1 teaspoon vanilla extract

Confectioners' sugar to taste

Warmed pancake syrup to taste

Yield: 8 to 10 servings

- Pour a mixture of the butter and brown sugar into a 9x13-inch baking dish.
- Layer the French bread over the top of the brown sugar mixture.
- Beat the eggs, milk and vanilla in a mixer bowl.
- Pour the egg mixture over the bread.
- Chill, covered, for 8 to 12 hours.
- Bake, uncovered, at 350 degrees for 45 minutes.
- Sprinkle with the confectioners' sugar and serve with the warmed pancake syrup.

Stuffed French Toast Strata

1 loaf French bread

8 ounces cream cheese

8 eggs

2½ cups milk or half-and-half

6 tablespoons melted butter or margarine

¼ cup maple syrup

Apple Cider Syrup to taste (page 43)

Yield: 8 to 10 servings

- Cut the French bread into cubes.
- Place half the bread cubes in a greased 9x13-inch baking dish.
- Cut the cream cheese into cubes.
- Layer the cream cheese cubes over the prepared layer.
- Top with the remaining bread cubes.
- Combine the eggs, milk, butter and syrup in a mixer bowl, beating until well blended.
- Pour the egg mixture over the prepared layers; press down to moisten.
- Chill, covered with plastic wrap, for 2 to 24 hours.
- Bake, uncovered, at 325 degrees for 25 to 40 minutes or until the edges are light golden brown and the center appears set.
- Let stand for 10 minutes before serving.
- Serve with the Apple Cider Syrup.

Till Midnight's Romano Herb Bread

People have driven to Holland from Chicago just to get a supply of this bread.

2 cups lukewarm water
3 tablespoons vegetable oil
3½ cups flour
2 envelopes yeast
2 teaspoons salt
2 teaspoons sugar
2 teaspoons dry milk
1½ cups grated Romano cheese
2 teaspoons garlic powder
2 teaspoons dry leaf basil
2 teaspoons Italian seasonings
1 egg white, beaten

Yield: 12 servings

- Combine the lukewarwm water, oil, flour, yeast, salt, sugar, dry milk, Romano cheese, garlic powder, basil and Italian seasonings in a large mixer bowl.
- Beat with an electric mixer fitted with dough hooks for 8 minutes.
- Knead the dough on a floured surface until smooth and elastic.
- Place the dough in a lightly oiled bowl, turning to coat the surface.
- Let rise, covered, for 20 to 30 minutes or until doubled in bulk.
- Punch the dough down.
- Divide the dough into 2 portions; shape each portion into a ball.
- Place the balls on a baking sheet dusted with cornmeal.
- Let rise, covered with plastic wrap, until almost doubled in bulk.
- Brush the dough with the beaten egg white.
- Bake at 375 degrees for 35 to 45 minutes or until the bread tests done.
- Cool on wire rack before cutting.
- *Note:* The bread is best baked on preheated 12x12-inch terra-cotta tiles or baking stones.

LEMON POPPY SEED PANCAKES
WITH RASPBERRY SYRUP

*I*f you're looking for something different, these are a great alternative to plain pancakes.

2 cups baking mix

1 cup milk

2 eggs

2 tablespoons poppy seeds

1 to 2 tablespoons lemon juice

Raspberry Syrup

RASPBERRY SYRUP

¼ cup orange juice

2 tablespoons honey

2 teaspoons cornstarch

1 cup frozen raspberries

Yield: 4 servings

- Use the baking mix package directions for pancakes, using the baking mix, milk and eggs and adding the poppy seeds and lemon juice.
- Bake on lightly greased hot griddle using package directions.
- Serve with Raspberry Syrup.

- Mix the orange juice, honey, cornstarch and raspberries in a medium saucepan.
- Cook over medium heat until bubbly, stirring constantly; do not overcook.

Puffy Pancake

*K*ids love these popover-style pancakes.

½ cup flour
½ cup milk
2 eggs, lightly beaten
Pinch of nutmeg
¼ cup butter
2 tablespoons confectioners' sugar
Juice of ½ lemon

Yield: 2 to 4 servings

- Beat the flour, milk, eggs and nutmeg lightly in a mixer bowl; batter will be slightly lumpy.
- Melt the butter in a 12-inch ovenproof skillet.
- Pour the batter into the hot skillet.
- Bake at 425 degrees for 15 to 20 minutes or until golden brown.
- Sprinkle with the confectioners' sugar; return to the oven for 1 minute.
- Sprinkle with the lemon juice.
- Serve with jelly, jam, fruit or syrup.

Apple Cider Syrup

¹/₂ cup sugar or apple cider
1 tablespoon cornstarch
¹/₂ teaspoon cinnamon
1 cup apple cider or apple juice
1 tablespoon lemon juice
2 tablespoons butter or margarine

Yield: 6 to 8 servings

- Combine the sugar, cornstarch and cinnamon in a small saucepan; mix well.
- Stir in the apple cider and lemon juice.
- Cook over medium heat until the mixture is thickened and bubbly, stirring constantly.
- Cook for 2 minutes longer, stirring constantly; remove from heat.
- Stir in the butter until melted.

Michigan Blueberry Syrup

Serve this syrup over pancakes, waffles or ice cream.

³/₄ cup water
2 cups sugar
1 tablespoon lemon juice
2 teaspoons cornstarch
1 tablespoon water
2 teaspoons quick-cooking tapioca
1 cup fresh blueberries

Yield: 4 to 6 servings

- Bring ³/₄ cup water and sugar to a boil in a saucepan over medium heat, stirring until the sugar dissolves.
- Stir in the lemon juice.
- Mix the cornstarch with 1 tablespoon water in a small bowl; add to the sugar mixture.
- Cook the sugar mixture over medium heat until clear and thickened, whisking constantly.
- Add the tapioca and blueberries.
- Cook for several minutes longer, stirring constantly.

THE LUNCH RUSH

AUTHENTIC 18TH AND 19TH CENTURY ARCHITECTURE
IS ON DISPLAY AT DUTCH VILLAGE

Horse and cart in a typical dutch village long ago.

Lois Lamb

The Lunch Rush

*Most requested recipe
from Eet Smakelijk

46

Chasen's Chili

8 ounces pinto beans
5 cups canned tomatoes
1 pound chopped green bell peppers
1¹/₂ tablespoons vegetable oil
1¹/₂ pounds chopped onions
2 cloves of garlic, crushed
¹/₂ cup chopped parsley
3¹/₂ pounds ground beef
¹/₂ cup butter
¹/₃ cup chili powder
2 tablespoons salt
1¹/₂ teaspoons pepper
1¹/₂ teaspoons cumin seeds

Yield: 10 to 12 servings

- Rinse and sort the beans.
- Soak the beans in water 2 inches above the beans in a bowl for 8 to 12 hours.
- Pour the beans with the water into a stockpot.
- Simmer, covered, for 2 hours or until the beans are tender.
- Add the tomatoes and simmer for 5 minutes longer.
- Sauté the green peppers in the oil in a skillet for 5 minutes, stirring frequently.
- Add the onions and sauté until tender, stirring frequently.
- Stir in the garlic and parsley.
- Brown the ground beef in the butter in a large skillet for 15 minutes, stirring until crumbly; drain.
- Add the ground beef to the onion mixture in the skillet.
- Stir in the chili powder; mix well.
- Simmer for 10 minutes.
- Stir the ground beef mixture into the bean mixture.
- Add the salt, pepper and cumin seeds.
- Simmer, covered, for 1 hour, stirring occasionally.
- Cook, uncovered, for 30 minutes, stirring occasionally.
- Let the chili cool slightly; skim the fat from the top.

Turkey and Black Bean Chili

1 pound ground turkey

$^{1}/_{2}$ cup chopped onion

2 (28-ounce) cans whole tomatoes

2 (15-ounce) cans black beans,
    rinsed, drained

1 (4-ounce) can chopped green chiles

1 tablespoon instant beef bouillon

$^{1}/_{4}$ teaspoon garlic powder

1 tablespoon chili powder

1 teaspoon ground cumin

Yield: 6 to 8 servings

- Brown the ground turkey with the onion in a stockpot, stirring until the turkey is crumbly; drain.
- Crush the undrained tomatoes; add to the turkey mixture.
- Stir in the beans, chiles, bouillon, garlic powder, chili powder and cumin; mix well.
- Bring the chili to a boil, stirring frequently; reduce heat.
- Simmer the chili over low heat for 30 minutes, stirring occasionally.
- *Note:* May use hot, medium or mild chiles.

White Chili

1 pound large white beans

6 cups chicken broth

2 cloves of garlic, minced

2 medium onions, chopped

1 tablespoon vegetable oil

2 (4-ounce) cans chopped green chiles

2 teaspoons ground cumin

2½ teaspoons dried oregano

¼ teaspoon ground cloves

¼ teaspoon cayenne

4 cups chopped cooked chicken breasts

3 cups shredded Monterey Jack cheese

Yield: 10 servings

- Bring the beans, chicken broth, garlic and half the onions to a boil in a large stockpot; reduce heat.
- Simmer for 3 hours or until the beans are tender; add more broth if necessary.
- Sauté the remaining onions in the oil in a skillet with the chiles, cumin, oregano, cloves and cayenne until the onions are tender.
- Add the onion mixture to the bean mixture; stir in the chicken.
- Simmer for 1 hour longer.
- Sprinkle the shredded cheese over the top before serving.

CAULIFLOWER SOUP

2 cups bite-size cauliflower pieces
1 (8-ounce) can chicken broth
1 (10-ounce) can cream of potato soup
1 cup milk
2 teaspoons cornstarch
White pepper to taste
Salt to taste
1/4 cup chopped shaved ham
Chopped parsley to taste
2 green onions, chopped
Grated Parmesan cheese to taste

Yield: 4 servings

- Cook the cauliflower, broth and soup in a saucepan over medium heat until the cauliflower is tender, stirring frequently.
- Add a mixture of the milk and cornstarch to the cauliflower.
- Stir in the white pepper, salt, ham, parsley and green onions.
- Cook the soup until heated through, stirring frequently.
- Sprinkle the Parmesan cheese over the top.

UIENSOEP*
(Easy Onion Soup)

12 medium onions, thinly sliced
1/2 cup (about) butter
1 quart beef stock
2 tablespoons flour
Salt and pepper to taste
4 slices bread, toasted

Yield: 4 servings

- Sauté the onions in the butter in a large saucepan until tender. Blend a small amount of the beef stock with the flour in a small bowl and set aside.
- Add the remaining stock to the onions. Bring to a simmer, stirring frequently.
- Stir the flour and stock mixture into the onion mixture. Cook until slightly thickened, stirring constantly. Season with salt and pepper.
- Place 1 slice bread in each of 4 soup bowls. Ladle the onion soup over the toast. Serve immediately.

Chicken Barley Soup with a Kick

Choose the strength of the kick with mild, medium or hot salsa.

2 cups chopped cooked
   chicken breasts

7 cups water

1 (16-ounce) jar salsa

1 onion, chopped

2 chicken bouillon cubes

1 cup chopped carrots

1 cup chopped celery

$^1/_2$ cup chopped green bell pepper

$^2/_3$ cup barley

Chopped parsley to taste

1 teaspoon salt

1 teaspoon pepper

1 teaspoon basil

$^1/_2$ teaspoon Worcestershire sauce

Yield: 6 servings

- Combine the chicken, water, salsa, onion and bouillon cubes in a large stockpot.
- Bring to a boil; reduce heat.
- Simmer for 1$^1/_2$ hours, stirring occasionally.
- Add the carrots, celery, green pepper and barley; mix well.
- Stir in the parsley, salt, pepper, basil and Worcestershire sauce.
- Simmer the soup until the vegetables are tender.

Sopa de Lima

4 boneless skinless chicken breast
   halves
1/2 bunch cilantro, chopped
10 black peppercorns
2 cloves of garlic, minced
3 to 4 quarts water
2 to 3 ears of corn
1 onion, chopped
1 cup margarine
3/4 cup flour
3 limes
Salt and pepper to taste
Chicken bouillon to taste

Yield: 8 servings

- Simmer the chicken, cilantro, peppercorns, garlic and water in a large stockpot for 2 hours, stirring occasionally.
- Remove the chicken from the stockpot with a slotted spoon.
- Chop into bite-size pieces.
- Strain the chicken stock through a sieve, reserving the stock.
- Cut the corn kernels from the ears of corn.
- Sauté the corn, chicken and onion in the margarine in a stockpot over medium heat for 2 to 3 minutes.
- Add the flour and cook for 2 minutes, stirring constantly.
- Add the reserved stock a small amount at a time, stirring constantly until the soup is smooth and adding more water if needed.
- Cut the limes into halves.
- Squeeze the lime juice into the soup, then add the limes.
- Add salt, pepper and bouillon; mix well.
- Simmer until the vegetables are tender and the flavors are blended.
- Discard the limes.
- Serve with crushed tortilla chips.
- *Note:* May use more lime if a more tangy taste is desired.

Chicken Tortilla Soup

½ cup chopped onion

1 teaspoon minced garlic

2 tablespoons butter

3 (14-ounce) cans chicken broth

1 (10-ounce) jar picante sauce

2 cups chopped cooked chicken
breasts

½ cup chopped red bell pepper

¼ teaspoon coarsely ground pepper

2 bay leaves

6 (6-inch) corn tortillas, cut into
½-inch wide strips

½ cup vegetable oil

2 avocados, peeled, cut into ½-inch
pieces

1 cup shredded Cheddar cheese

¼ cup sour cream

Yield: 6 servings

- Sauté the onion and garlic in the butter in a stockpot over medium heat until the onion is tender.
- Add the broth, picante sauce, chicken, red pepper, pepper and bay leaves.
- Bring to a boil; reduce heat.
- Simmer, covered, for 20 minutes, stirring occasionally.
- Discard the bay leaves.
- Fry the tortilla strips in the oil in a large skillet over medium heat until light golden brown; drain on paper towels.
- Place an equal amount of tortilla strips in 6 soup bowls.
- Ladle the soup over the strips.
- Top with the avocados, Cheddar cheese and sour cream.

Quick Corn Chowder

2 cups chopped peeled potatoes
1/2 cup chopped carrot
1/2 cup chopped celery
1/4 cup chopped onion
1/2 teaspoon pepper
2 cups water
1/4 cup butter
1/4 cup flour
2 cups milk
1 cup freshly grated Parmesan cheese
1 (8-ounce) can cream-style corn

Yield: 4 servings

- Combine the potatoes, carrot, celery, onion, pepper and water in a saucepan.
- Bring to a boil; reduce heat.
- Simmer, covered, for 10 minutes.
- Melt the butter in a saucepan.
- Stir in the flour and the milk; mix well.
- Cook over medium heat until thick and bubbly, stirring constantly; cook for 1 minute longer.
- Add the cheese, stirring until melted.
- Add the cheese mixture to the vegetables.
- Mix in the corn.
- Cook until heated through, stirring constantly.

Summer Cucumber Soup

*M*ake ahead and refrigerate for a lovely bridal luncheon.

3 cucumbers, peeled, seeded
3 cups chicken broth
3 cups sour cream
3 tablespoons cider vinegar
1 clove of garlic, minced
2 tablespoons dill
2 teaspoons salt

Yield: 4 servings

- Grate the cucumbers; drain and squeeze out all the liquid.
- Place the grated cucumbers in a large bowl.
- Add the chicken broth, sour cream, vinegar, garlic, dill and salt; mix well.
- Chill until serving time.
- Garnish with chopped parsley, chopped tomatoes, chopped scallions and dollops of sour cream.
- *Note:* May substitute nonfat yogurt for sour cream.

Kerry Soep*
(Curry Soup)

4 cups beef stock

2 cloves

1 bay leaf

1 small red pepper

1 large onion, chopped

1 teaspoon curry

2¹/₂ tablespoons butter

¹/₄ cup flour

1 egg, beaten

Yield: 4 servings

- Boil the beef stock, cloves, bay leaf and red pepper in a saucepan; strain, reserving the liquid.
- Sauté the onion and curry in the butter in a saucepan; add the flour.
- Add the beef stock gradually, stirring constantly.
- Boil for 10 minutes, stirring occasionally.
- Stir a small amount of the hot mixture into the beaten egg; stir the egg mixture into the hot mixture.
- Strain the soup again if desired.
- Serve with croutons, meatballs or chopped hard-cooked eggs.
- *Note:* May substitute 4 cups water and 4 to 5 beef bouillon cubes for the beef stock.

Dill Pickle Soup

Wonderful served with a green salad and crusty bread.

5 carrots, sliced
3 potatoes, peeled, chopped
3 stalks celery, sliced
1 pound ground beef
1/4 cup chopped onion
1/2 cup rolled oats
1 egg
Salt and pepper to taste
5 dill pickle spears, sliced
2 teaspoons dried dillweed
1 tablespoon salt
1/4 teaspoon pepper
1/4 cup dill pickle juice
2 tablespoons flour
1/2 cup sour cream

Yield: 4 servings

- Bring the carrots, potatoes and celery to a boil in water to cover in a stockpot; reduce heat.
- Simmer for 15 minutes.
- Combine the ground beef, onion, oats, egg and salt and pepper to taste in a bowl; mix well.
- Shape the ground beef mixture into meatballs.
- Drop the meatballs into the simmering vegetable mixture.
- Cook for 20 minutes.
- Add the pickle slices, dillweed, 1 tablespoon salt, 1/4 teaspoon pepper and pickle juice.
- Blend the flour and sour cream in a small bowl.
- Stir a small amount of the hot mixture into the sour cream mixture; stir the sour cream mixture into the hot mixture.
- Heat until the soup is slightly thickened; do not boil.

Dutch Pea Soup*
(Erwtensoep)

1 pound dried peas
1 medium ham hock, shoulder pork
   or mettwurst
3 quarts water
Salt and pepper to taste
1½ cups chopped celery
3 medium onions, chopped
3 potatoes, chopped
2 carrots, chopped
Parsley to taste
1 cup milk

Yield: 6 servings

- Sort and rinse peas.
- Soak the peas in cold water to cover in a bowl for 8 to 12 hours; drain.
- Cook the ham hock, peas and water in a saucepan over medium heat for 2 hours.
- Add salt, pepper, celery, onions, potatoes and carrots; mix gently.
- Cook for 1 hour longer; add the parsley and milk.
- Cook over low heat for 10 minutes longer or until heated through.

Very Mushroom Soup

A meal in itself when served with a crusty brown bread.

1 pound fresh mushrooms

1³/₄ cups chopped onions

¹/₂ teaspoon sugar

¹/₂ cup butter

¹/₄ cup flour

1 cup water

2 (10-ounce) cans low-sodium
   chicken broth

³/₄ cup dry vermouth

2 teaspoons salt

¹/₄ teaspoon pepper

Yield: 4 to 6 servings

- Slice ¹/₃ of the mushrooms; chop the remaining mushrooms.
- Sauté the onions and sugar in the butter in a large stockpot over medium heat until the onions are tender.
- Add the mushrooms.
- Sauté for 5 minutes.
- Stir in the flour until the mixture is smooth.
- Cook for 2 minutes, stirring constantly.
- Pour in the water, stirring until smooth.
- Add the broth, vermouth, salt and pepper; mix well.
- Bring to a boil, stirring constantly; reduce heat.
- Simmer for 10 minutes.

Hearty Potato Soup

Place small bowls of parsley, crumbled bacon and croutons on the table and let everyone top their bowls as desired.

6 medium potatoes, peeled, chopped

2 carrots, sliced

6 stalks celery, chopped

1 medium onion, chopped

3 cups water

6 tablespoons margarine

3 tablespoons flour

Salt and pepper to taste

1½ cups milk

8 ounces cream cheese, softened

1 (10-ounce) can cream of chicken soup

Yield: 6 servings

- Cook the potatoes, carrots, celery and onion in the water in a stockpot until tender.
- Melt the margarine in a saucepan.
- Stir in the flour, salt and pepper.
- Add the milk gradually, stirring until thickened.
- Add the cream cheese and soup, stirring until smooth.
- Add the cream cheese mixture to the vegetables.
- Cook over low heat until heated through.
- *Note:* Additional water may be added for a thinner soup.

Autumn Butternut Squash Soup

2 medium butternut squash
4 cups chicken broth
4 cups whipping cream
½ cup packed brown sugar
1 tablespoon cinnamon
¼ teaspoon nutmeg
Salt and white pepper to taste

Yield: 6 servings

- Cut the squash into halves lengthwise.
- Place the squash cut side down on a baking sheet.
- Bake at 350 degrees for 1 hour.
- Purée the squash, reserving 4 cups.
- Combine the broth, whipping cream, 4 cups squash and brown sugar in a large saucepan; mix well.
- Add the cinnamon, nutmeg, salt and white pepper.
- Cook over low heat until heated through.

Tamale Soup

*F*ruit salad and bread are nice complements to this spicy soup.

2 pounds ground beef

2 onions, chopped

2 green bell peppers, chopped

1 tablespoon vegetable oil

2 tablespoons garlic powder

2 tablespoons chili powder, or
   to taste

1 envelope taco seasoning mix

1 1/2 teaspoons seasoned salt

1 (15-ounce) can kidney beans

1 (11-ounce) can niblet corn

1 (6-ounce) can whole black olives,
   cut into halves

4 cups beef broth

2 (28-ounce) cans stewed tomatoes

1 (4-ounce) can chopped green chiles

6 small flour tortillas, cut into 3/4-inch
   pieces

Yield: 6 servings

- Sauté the ground beef, onions and green peppers in the oil in a large saucepan, stirring until the ground beef is crumbly and cooked through and the vegetables are tender.
- Add the garlic powder, chili powder, taco mix and seasoned salt; mix well.
- Stir in the undrained beans, corn, olives, beef broth, tomatoes and chiles.
- Stir the tortilla pieces into the soup; simmer for 30 minutes.
- Ladle the soup into soup bowls; garnish with a dollop of sour cream and shredded Cheddar cheese.

After-Work Minestrone

For a quick, delicious meal, serve this minestrone with a green salad and crusty bread.

2 to 3 cloves of fresh garlic, minced

2 tablespoons olive oil

1 cup chopped onion

1 cup chopped carrot

1 cup chopped celery

1 cup green beans, cut into 1-inch pieces

4 cups water

1 (28-ounce) can crushed tomatoes

1/2 cup uncooked macaroni

1 (15-ounce) can Great Northern beans

1 cup chopped fresh spinach

Salt and pepper to taste

Grated Parmesan cheese to taste

Yield: 4 to 6 servings

- Sauté the garlic in the olive oil in a large saucepan.
- Add the onion, carrot, celery, green beans, water and tomatoes; mix well.
- Cook over low heat for 40 minutes, stirring occasionally.
- Add the macaroni, Great Northern beans, spinach, salt and pepper.
- Cook until the macaroni is tender.
- Ladle into soup bowls; sprinkle with Parmesan cheese.

Asparagus Pasta Salad

1 pound asparagus, cut into 1-inch
  pieces
1 (8-ounce) package vermicelli
3/4 cup mayonnaise
Juice of 1 small lemon
1 teaspoon garlic powder
1/2 teaspoon celery salt
1/2 teaspoon basil
1/4 teaspoon Beau Monde seasoning
1/4 teaspoon pepper
1 tomato, chopped
4 green onions, chopped
1 (4-ounce) can sliced black olives
4 ounces boiled ham, chopped
1 cup shredded mild white cheese
1/3 cup grated Parmesan cheese
1 tablespoon chopped parsley
1 teaspoon chopped chives
  (optional)

Yield: 4 to 6 servings

- Boil or steam the asparagus in a saucepan for 3 to 4 minutes; drain.
- Let the asparagus stand until cool.
- Break the vermicelli into halves.
- Cook until al dente using package directions; drain.
- Let the vermicelli stand until cool.
- Combine the mayonnaise, lemon juice, garlic powder, celery salt, basil, Beau Monde seasoning and pepper in a small bowl.
- Combine the vermicelli, asparagus, tomato, green onions, olives, ham, white cheese, Parmesan cheese, parsley and chives in a large serving bowl.
- Pour the mayonnaise sauce over the top, tossing to coat.
- Chill until serving time.

Broccoli Salad

1 bunch broccoli, cut into small pieces

1 small red onion, chopped

1 cup shredded Cheddar cheese

8 ounces bacon, crisp-fried, crumbled

3 ounces spinach fettuccini, cooked, drained

$^{1}/_{4}$ cup sugar

$^{1}/_{2}$ cup mayonnaise

1 tablespoon vinegar

Yield: 4 servings

- Combine the broccoli, onion, Cheddar cheese and bacon in a serving bowl, tossing until mixed.
- Add the fettuccini; toss and set aside.
- Combine the sugar, mayonnaise and vinegar in a small bowl; mix well.
- Spoon over the broccoli mixture, tossing to coat.
- Chill until serving time.

Chinese Chicken Salad

2 (3-ounce) packages ramen noodles
  with chicken-flavor seasoning

1 head cabbage, chopped

6 to 8 green onions, sliced

1 cup toasted slivered almonds

1/2 cup sesame seeds

1 bunch cilantro

4 boneless skinless chicken breasts,
  cooked, chopped

1/4 cup sugar

2 teaspoons salt

1 cup vegetable oil

1/4 cup vinegar

Yield: 4 to 6 servings

- Crumble the ramen noodles into a serving bowl, tossing with the chicken-flavor seasoning.
- Add the cabbage, green onions, almonds, sesame seeds, cilantro and chicken.
- Combine the sugar, salt, oil and vinegar in a jar with a lid; shake until well mixed.
- Pour the sugar mixture over the cabbage mixture just before serving, tossing to coat.

GREAT GRAPE CHICKEN SALAD

This salad, along with croissants and fresh fruit, makes an ideal picnic lunch.

4 cups chopped cooked chicken

2 cups seedless green grapes

2 cups chopped celery

1 small onion, chopped

2 cups mayonnaise

1 teaspoon poppy seeds

1 teaspoon salt

1/2 teaspoon cracked black pepper

1/2 teaspoon poultry seasoning

1/2 cup sliced almonds

Yield: 4 to 6 servings

- Combine the chicken, grapes, celery and onion in a large serving bowl.
- Add a mixture of the mayonnaise, poppy seeds, salt, pepper, poultry seasoning and almonds, tossing to coat.
- Chill for 8 to 12 hours.

CHICKEN SALAD WITH A TWIST

This recipe may easily be doubled to serve a crowd.

4 cups chopped cooked chicken

2 cups chopped celery

1 (8-ounce) can artichoke hearts, drained, chopped

1/2 cup coarsely chopped pecans

4 slices bacon, crisp-fried, crumbled

1 cup green olives, sliced

1/2 cup rotini, cooked, drained

1 cup sour cream

1 1/2 teaspoons salt

2 tablespoons lemon juice

1 cup mayonnaise

Yield: 4 to 6 servings

- Combine the chicken, celery, artichokes, pecans, bacon, olives and rotini in a salad bowl, tossing to mix.
- Mix the sour cream, salt, lemon juice and mayonnaise in a small bowl, stirring until smooth.
- Spoon over chicken mixture, tossing lightly to coat.
- Chill until serving time.

Shrimp in Green Sauce

2 slices white bread, crusts removed

1/2 cup red wine vinegar

3 cups packed parsley with stems removed

3 tablespoons drained rinsed capers

3 cloves of garlic, crushed

4 anchovy fillets

3/4 cup olive oil

2 pounds large or jumbo shrimp, cooked, peeled, halved

Yield: 8 servings

- Soak the bread in the vinegar in a shallow bowl for 10 minutes.
- Squeeze the bread dry.
- Combine the bread, parsley, capers, garlic and anchovies in a food processor container.
- Add the olive oil in a fine stream, processing constantly until blended.
- Pour over the shrimp in a serving bowl, tossing to coat.
- May serve on Bibb or Boston lettuce topped with sliced tomatoes.

Shrimp Pita Salad

2 cups chilled, chopped, cooked shrimp

$^1/_2$ cup finely chopped celery

Chopped green onions to taste

Juice of 1 lemon

$^3/_4$ cup chilled mayonnaise

Pinch of curry powder

Ground pepper to taste

1 head iceberg or romaine lettuce,
    torn into bite-size pieces

4 pita bread rounds

Yield: 4 servings

- Combine the shrimp, celery and green onions in a chilled bowl.
- Add the lemon juice, mayonnaise and curry powder; mix gently.
- Sprinkle with pepper.
- Arrange the lettuce on 4 salad plates.
- Mound the shrimp salad in the center of the lettuce.
- Cut each pita round into 8 wedges.
- Arrange the pita wedges with points out around the shrimp salad.
- *Note:* May cut each pita round into halves and fill each half with the lettuce and the shrimp salad, serving on a chilled plate garnished with fresh fruit.

Tea Time

Cappon House, historic home of industrialist Issac Cappon

*My thoughts were of the days when the Cappon house
was in its glory. I wondered how people lived
and entertained. I imagined ladies in long skirts, with
horses and buggies passing by.*

Lois Lamb

Tea Time

*Most requested recipe
from **Eet Smakelijk**

Banana Nut Muffins

1 1/2 cups flour

1 1/2 teaspoons baking soda

1/4 teaspoon salt

1/8 teaspoon ground nutmeg

1 1/4 cups mashed bananas

1/2 cup each sugar and unsalted butter

1/4 cup packed brown sugar

1/4 cup milk

1 egg

1 cup unsalted macadamia nuts,
   toasted, chopped

Yield: 12 muffins

- Sift the flour, baking soda, salt and nutmeg together into a large bowl.
- Combine the bananas, sugar, butter, brown sugar, milk and egg in a bowl; mix well.
- Stir into the flour mixture. Fold in half of the macadamia nuts. Divide the batter evenly into 12 greased muffin cups. Sprinkle with the remaining macadamia nuts.
- Bake at 350 degrees for 25 minutes or until golden brown and muffins test done. Remove to a wire rack to cool.

Bran Muffins

2 cups boiling water

2 cups bran cereal

4 cups Bran Buds cereal

5 teaspoons baking soda

1 quart buttermilk

3 cups sugar

1 cup shortening

5 cups flour

1 tablespoon salt

4 eggs, slightly beaten

Yield: 60 muffins

- Pour the boiling water over bran cereal and Bran Buds cereal in a large bowl. Let stand until cool.
- Dissolve the baking soda in the buttermilk in a bowl.
- Cream the sugar and shortening in a mixer bowl until light and fluffy.
- Add the flour, salt, eggs and buttermilk mixture; mix well. Stir in the cereal mixture. Fill greased muffin cups 2/3 full.
- Bake at 375 degrees for 20 minutes or until muffins test done. Remove to a wire rack to cool. The batter may be stored in the refrigerator for 6 to 8 weeks.

Michigan Blueberry Muffins

Holland has acres and acres of blueberry fields.

3/4 cup sugar

1/4 cup margarine, softened

2 eggs

2 cups flour

2 teaspoons baking powder

1/4 teaspoon salt

1/2 cup milk

2 cups fresh blueberries

1/4 cup margarine, softened

1/2 cup sugar

1/3 cup flour

1/2 teaspoon cinnamon

Yield: 12 muffins

- Cream 3/4 cup sugar and 1/4 cup margarine in a mixer bowl until light and fluffy.
- Beat in the eggs one at a time.
- Mix 2 cups flour, baking powder and salt together.
- Add to the creamed mixture alternately with the milk, beating well after each addition.
- Fold in the blueberries.
- Line the muffin cups with paper liners.
- Fill the muffin cups 3/4 full.
- Mix the 1/4 cup margarine, 1/2 cup sugar, 1/3 cup flour and the cinnamon together in a bowl.
- Sprinkle over the muffin batter.
- Bake at 350 degrees for 18 to 20 minutes or until the muffins test done.
- Serve warm.

Very Berry Muffins

Enjoy the tastes of summer.

2 cups flour

¹/₂ cup sugar

1 tablespoon baking powder

2 teaspoons each grated lemon and
    orange peel

¹/₂ teaspoon salt

¹/₂ cup orange juice

¹/₂ cup melted butter or margarine

1 egg

³/₄ cup fresh blueberries

³/₄ cup fresh raspberries

Yield: 12 large muffins

- Combine the flour, sugar, baking powder, lemon peel, orange peel and salt in a bowl; mix well.
- Mix the orange juice, melted butter and egg together in a bowl.
- Add to the dry ingredients, stirring until moistened.
- The batter will be very thick.
- Fold the blueberries and raspberries gently into the mixture.
- Spray the muffin cups with nonstick baking spray or line with paper liners.
- Fill the muffin cups ³/₄ full.
- Bake at 400 degrees for 18 to 25 minutes or until golden brown.
- Cool in the pan for 1 minute.
- Remove to a wire rack.

CRANBERRY MUFFINS

A wonderful treat to unwind with after a day of holiday shopping.

½ cup butter or margarine, softened
1¼ cups sugar
2 eggs
1 cup reduced-fat sour cream
1 teaspoon vanilla extract
2 cups flour
1 teaspoon baking powder
½ teaspoon baking soda
1½ cups dried cranberries
⅓ cup flour
¼ cup sugar
2 tablespoons butter or margarine, softened
½ teaspoon cinnamon
¼ cup walnuts, finely chopped

Yield: 12 muffins

- Cream ½ cup butter and 1¼ cups sugar in a mixer bowl until light and fluffy.
- Beat in the eggs 1 at a time.
- Add the sour cream and vanilla; mix well.
- Mix 2 cups flour, baking powder and baking soda together.
- Add to the creamed mixture; mix well.
- Fold in the cranberries.
- Spoon into greased muffin cups.
- Mix ⅓ cup flour, ¼ cup sugar, 2 tablespoons butter and cinnamon in a bowl.
- Stir in the walnuts.
- Sprinkle the cinnamon mixture over the batter in each muffin cup; swirl into the batter with a knife to marbelize.
- Bake at 400 degrees for 20 to 25 minutes or until the muffins test done.
- Remove to a wire rack to cool.

Butterscotch Pumpkin Muffins

A hit with all ages.

1 cup all-purpose flour
3/4 cup whole wheat flour
1/2 cup packed brown sugar
1/2 cup sugar
1/2 teaspoon ginger
1/2 teaspoon mace
1 teaspoon cinnamon
1/8 teaspoon ground cloves
1 teaspoon baking soda
1/4 teaspoon baking powder
1/4 teaspoon salt
2 eggs
1 cup canned pumpkin
1/2 cup melted butter
1 cup butterscotch chips
1/2 cup chopped pecans (optional)

Yield: 24 muffins

- Combine the all-purpose flour, whole wheat flour, brown sugar, sugar, ginger, mace, cinnamon, cloves, baking soda, baking powder and salt in a large bowl; mix well.
- Make a well in the center.
- Whisk the eggs, pumpkin and melted butter in a bowl.
- Stir in the butterscotch chips and pecans.
- Add to the dry ingredients, mixing just until moistened; do not overmix.
- Spoon the batter into greased muffin cups.
- Bake at 350 degrees for 20 to 25 minutes or until muffins test done.
- Remove to a wire rack to cool.

Pumpkin Muffins

2 cups sugar

5 cups vegetable oil

3 eggs

1½ cups canned pumpkin

5 cups water

3 cups flour

1½ teaspoons baking powder

1 teaspoon baking soda

1 teaspoon salt

1 teaspoon cinnamon

½ teaspoon cloves

½ teaspoon nutmeg

1½ cups raisins

1 cup chopped walnuts

Yield: 24 muffins

- Cream the sugar and oil in a mixer bowl.
- Beat in the eggs 1 at a time.
- Add the pumpkin and water; mix well.
- Mix the flour, baking powder, baking soda, salt, cinnamon, cloves and nutmeg together.
- Add to the pumpkin mixture, stirring until well blended.
- Fold in the raisins and walnuts.
- Let stand at room temperature for 1 hour.
- Spoon into greased muffins cups.
- Bake at 400 degrees for 15 minutes or until muffins test done.
- Remove to a wire rack to cool.

Bran Scones

1 cup whole bran cereal

1/2 cup buttermilk

1 egg, beaten

1 egg white

1 tablespoon melted butter

3 packages biscuit mix

1/2 cup sugar

1 teaspoon cinnamon

1 egg yolk

1 tablespoon milk

1 tablespoon sugar

Yield: 16 scones

- Combine the cereal and buttermilk in a bowl. Let stand for 3 minutes or until the milk is absorbed. Stir in the egg, egg white and melted butter.
- Combine the biscuit mix, 1/2 cup sugar and cinnamon in a bowl. Make a well in the center and add the bran mixture, stirring just until mixed. Turn onto a floured surface. Knead gently 10 to 15 times or until smooth and elastic. Divide the dough into 2 equal portions. Pat each portion into a circle on a large greased baking sheet. Cut each circle into 8 wedges.
- Mix the egg yolk, milk and 1 tablespoon sugar in a bowl. Brush over the top of each scone.
- Bake at 425 degrees for 12 to 14 minutes or until golden brown. Serve warm.

Amandel Koekjes*
(Almond Paste Cookies)

1/2 cup each butter and margarine, softened

3/4 cup sugar

2 eggs

1 1/2 cups flour

1/2 teaspoon baking soda

1 cup almond or kernel paste

1/2 cup chopped almonds

Yield: 36 cookies

- Cream the butter, margarine and sugar in a mixer bowl until light and fluffy. Beat in eggs 1 at a time.
- Add a mixture of flour and baking soda. Add the almond paste. Add a few drops of water if dough is too stiff. Stir in the almonds. Drop by teaspoonfuls onto a greased cookie sheet.
- Bake at 325 degrees for 15 minutes or until brown. Cool on a wire rack.

Caramel Apple Cookies

³/₄ cup confectioners' sugar

²/₃ cup margarine, softened

3 tablespoons frozen apple juice concentrate, thawed

1¹/₂ cups flour

¹/₄ teaspoon salt

30 caramel candies

2 tablespoons water

³/₄ cup finely chopped walnuts

Yield: 12 to 18 cookies

- Cream the confectioners' sugar and margarine in a mixer bowl until light and fluffy.
- Add 1 tablespoon of the apple juice concentrate; mix well.
- Add the flour and salt; mix well.
- Shape the mixture into ³/₄-inch balls.
- Place on a nonstick cookie sheet.
- Bake at 350 degrees for 12 to 17 minutes or until light brown.
- Insert a wooden pick into the center of each cookie immediately.
- Cool completely.
- Combine the caramel candies, water and remaining apple juice concentrate in a saucepan.
- Cook over low heat until caramel candies are melted, stirring frequently until mixture is smooth.
- Spread the walnuts on a flat surface.
- Spoon the caramel mixture over all sides of each cookie and press the bottom of the cookie into the walnuts.
- Place the cookies on waxed paper.
- Let stand until firm.

Double Chocolate Biscotti

4 ounces unsweetened chocolate

4 teaspoons butter

3 eggs

1 cup sugar

2 cups flour

2 teaspoons baking powder

1/8 teaspoon salt

1 cup chopped walnuts

2 cups chocolate chips

Yield: 50 servings

- Melt the unsweetened chocolate and butter in a saucepan over low heat.
- Beat the eggs and sugar in a mixer bowl until frothy.
- Add the chocolate mixture; mix well.
- Mix the flour, baking powder and salt together.
- Add to the chocolate mixture; beat well.
- Fold in the walnuts and chocolate chips.
- Divide the dough into 3 portions.
- Wrap each in plastic wrap.
- Chill for 1 hour.
- Shape each portion of dough into a 9-inch log with lightly floured hands.
- Arrange horizontally 3 inches apart on an ungreased cookie sheet.
- Press each log to flatten to 2 inches.
- Bake at 350 degrees for 30 minutes.
- Remove logs to a cutting board with a spatula.
- Cut each log into a 1/2-inch diagonal slice with a serrated knife.
- Arrange slices upright on the cookie sheet.
- Bake for 20 minutes longer.
- Cool on a wire rack.

Susan Bartolomei's Almond-Apricot Biscotti

A new take on the classic Italian crunchy cookie. The biscotti keep well and look great wrapped in tinted cellophane and tied with French silk ribbon or packed into holiday bags.

2³/₄ cups sifted flour

1¹/₂ cups sugar

¹/₂ cup chilled unsalted butter, cut into pieces

2¹/₂ teaspoons baking powder

1 teaspoon salt

1 teaspoon ground ginger

3¹/₂ ounces white chocolate, cut into pieces

1²/₃ cups whole almonds, toasted

2 large eggs

¹/₄ cup plus 1 tablespoon apricot-flavored brandy

2 teaspoons almond extract

1 (6-ounce) package dried apricots, finely chopped

Yield: 40 biscotti

- Line a 12x18-inch cookie sheet with foil. Butter and flour the foil.
- Process the flour, sugar, butter, baking powder, salt and ginger in a food processor until crumbly.
- Add the white chocolate. Process until finely chopped. Add the toasted almonds; chop coarsely by pulsing 6 to 8 times.
- Beat the eggs, brandy and almond flavoring together in a mixer bowl until well blended.
- Add the flour mixture and apricots, stirring until a stiff dough forms.
- Drop dough by spoonfuls into three 12-inch long strips on prepared cookie sheet, spacing evenly. Moisten fingertips and shape dough into 2-inch wide logs. Chill for 30 minutes or until dough is firm.
- Bake at 350 degrees on center oven rack for 30 minutes or until golden brown. Place cookie sheet on wire rack and cool completely.
- Cut each log crosswise into ³/₄-inch slices. Place the cookies cut side down on a greased cookie sheet. Reduce oven temperature to 300 degrees.
- Bake for 10 minutes. Turn cookies over. Bake for 10 minutes longer. Remove to wire rack to cool.

Peanut Butter and Chocolate Layered Brownies

4 squares unsweetened chocolate

³/4 cup butter

2 cups sugar

3 eggs

1 teaspoon vanilla extract

1 cup flour

1¹/2 cups peanut butter

1 teaspoon vanilla extract

³/4 cup confectioners' sugar

4 squares semisweet chocolate

¹/4 cup butter

Yield: 15 servings

- Melt the unsweetened chocolate and ³/4 cup butter in a saucepan over low heat, stirring frequently.
- Stir in the sugar.
- Add the eggs, 1 teaspoon vanilla and flour; mix well.
- Spread into a greased 9x13-inch baking pan.
- Bake at 350 degrees for 30 to 35 minutes or until brownies pull from the sides of the pan.
- Place baking pan on a wire rack to cool.
- Cream the peanut butter, 1 teaspoon vanilla and confectioners' sugar in a mixer bowl until smooth.
- Spread over the cooled brownies.
- Melt the semisweet chocolate and ¹/4 cup butter in a saucepan over low heat, stirring frequently.
- Spread over the peanut butter layer.
- Cool until set.
- Cut into squares.

One-Pot Brownies*

If you've been searching for the ultimate brownie, look no further.

4 (1-ounce) squares unsweetened
   chocolate
1 cup margarine
2 cups sugar
4 eggs
1½ cups flour
2 teaspoons vanilla extract
1 cup chopped walnuts
1 cup raisins (optional)

Yield: 24 servings

- Melt the unsweetened chocolate and margarine in a heavy saucepan over low heat, stirring frequently. Cool slightly.
- Add the sugar and eggs; mix well.
- Beat in the flour and vanilla. Stir in the walnuts and raisins. Pour into a greased baking pan.
- Bake at 375 degrees for 20 to 25 minutes or until brownies pull from the sides of the pan.
- Do not overbake. Cool slightly. Cut into squares while still warm.

Krakelingen*
(Figure Eight-Shaped Butter Cookies)

2 cups butter
4 cups flour
½ cup water
1 cup sugar

Yield: 72 cookies

- Cut the butter into the flour in a bowl.
- Add the water gradually, mixing until the dough resembles pie pastry. Chill, covered, overnight.
- Roll the dough a small amount at a time into a pencil shape; bring ends together and twist into a "figure eight." Dip both sides in sugar; place on a nonstick cookie sheet.
- Bake at 375 degrees until cookies are brown on the bottom. Cool on a wire rack.

Everyone's Favorite Chocolate Chip Cookies

The best of the best!

1 cup unsalted butter, softened

1 cup sugar

1 cup packed brown sugar

2 eggs, at room temperature

2¹/₂ cups rolled oats

¹/₂ teaspoon salt

1 teaspoon baking powder

1 teaspoon baking soda

2 cups flour

1 teaspoon vanilla extract

2 cups large gourmet chocolate chips
   or white chocolate chunks

1 (8-ounce) milk chocolate bar, grated

1¹/₂ cups chopped walnuts or
   macadamia nuts

Yield: 24 cookies

- Cream the butter, sugar and brown sugar in a mixer bowl until light and fluffy.
- Beat in the eggs 1 at a time.
- Process the oats in a food processor until powdered.
- Add to the creamed mixture.
- Sift the salt, baking powder, baking soda and flour together.
- Add to the creamed mixture; mix well.
- Stir in the vanilla, chocolate chips, grated chocolate and walnuts.
- Shape into 1-inch balls.
- Place on nonstick cookie sheets.
- Do not flatten.
- Bake at 400 degrees for 8 minutes.
- Do not overbake; cookies will not appear fully baked.
- Cool on the cookie sheets.
- Remove to wire racks to cool completely.

Cowboy Cookies

2¼ cups sugar

2¼ cups packed brown sugar

2¼ cups shortening

5 eggs

2¼ teaspoons vanilla extract

4½ cups flour

2¼ teaspoons baking soda

1⅛ teaspoons baking powder

1⅛ teaspoons salt

4½ cups rolled oats

4 cups chocolate chips

1 cup chopped walnuts

Yield: 30 cookies

- Cream the sugar, brown sugar and shortening in a mixer bowl until light and fluffy.
- Beat in the eggs 1 at a time. Add the vanilla.
- Combine the flour, baking soda, baking powder, salt and oats in a bowl; mix well.
- Add to the creamed mixture.
- Stir in the chocolate chips and walnuts.
- Drop the batter onto a nonstick cookie sheet by small ice cream scoopfuls for uniform size cookies.
- Bake at 350 degrees for 15 minutes or until the cookies are light brown.
- Cool on a wire rack.

Crispy Date Bars

1 cup flour

1/2 cup packed brown sugar

1/2 cup margarine, softened

1 cup chopped dates

1/2 cup sugar

1/2 cup margarine, softened

1 egg, beaten

2 cups crisp rice cereal

1 cup chopped walnuts

1 teaspoon vanilla extract

2 cups confectioners' sugar

1/2 teaspoon vanilla extract

3 ounces cream cheese, softened

Yield: 15 bars

- Mix the flour and brown sugar in a bowl.
- Cut in 1/2 cup margarine until mixture is crumbly.
- Press over the bottom of a greased 9x13-inch baking pan.
- Bake at 375 degrees for 10 to 12 minutes or until brown.
- Combine the dates, sugar and 1/2 cup margarine in a medium saucepan.
- Bring to a boil over medium heat, stirring constantly; reduce heat.
- Simmer for 3 minutes, stirring constantly.
- Stir about 1/4 cup of the mixture into the beaten egg.
- Stir the egg into the hot mixture.
- Cook until the mixture bubbles, stirring constantly.
- Remove from heat; let stand until cool.
- Stir in the rice cereal, walnuts and 1 teaspoon vanilla.
- Spread over the baked layer; cool.
- Beat the confectioners' sugar, 1/2 teaspoon vanilla and cream cheese in a mixer bowl until smooth.
- Spread over the top.
- Cut into bars.

De Zwaan Koekjes*
(Windmill Cookies)

1 cup chopped dates
¹/₂ cup sugar
¹/₂ cup water
2 tablespoons lemon juice
¹/₂ teaspoon salt
2 cups packed brown sugar
1 cup melted shortening
2 eggs, beaten
1 cup sour milk
2 cups whole wheat (graham) flour
2¹/₂ cups all-purpose flour
¹/₂ teaspoon baking soda
1 teaspoon cinnamon

Yield: 24 cookies

- Combine the dates, sugar and water in a saucepan over medium heat.
- Simmer for 5 minutes or until thickened, stirring frequently.
- Stir in the lemon juice and salt.
- Remove from the heat.
- Beat the brown sugar and shortening in a mixer bowl until light and fluffy.
- Add the eggs and sour milk; mix well.
- Sift the whole wheat flour, all-purpose flour, baking soda and cinnamon together.
- Add to the brown sugar mixture; mix well.
- Add additional flour if needed for a dough stiff enough to roll.
- Roll the dough ¹/₈ inch thick on a floured surface.
- Cut with a round cookie cutter.
- Place ¹/₂ of the rounds on a greased cookie sheet; top each with a spoonful of the date mixture.
- Cut 4 small slits into each remaining round to resemble windmill sails.
- Place over the date mixture.
- Bake at 375 degrees for 10 minutes.
- Cool on a wire rack.

Jan Hagel*

Sugar cookies—very delicate!

¹/₂ cup butter, softened

¹/₂ cup margarine, softened

³/₄ cup sugar

1 egg yolk

2 cups flour

1 teaspoon cinnamon

¹/₄ teaspoon baking soda

1 egg white, slightly beaten

1 cup sliced almonds

Yield: 72 cookies

- Cream the butter, margarine and sugar in a mixer bowl until light and fluffy. Add the egg yolk; mix well.
- Sift the flour, cinnamon and baking soda together. Add to the creamed mixture; mix well. Add a few drops of water if dough is too thick. Divide the dough into 2 equal portions. Place each portion in the center of a greased cookie sheet, pressing with hands to flatten.
- Place a sheet of waxed paper over the dough; roll very thin. Remove the waxed paper and brush the dough with slightly beaten egg white. Sprinkle with almonds, pressing the almonds into dough.
- Bake at 325 degrees for 25 minutes. Cut immediately into bars; remove to a wire rack to cool.

Molasses Cookies

³/₄ cup shortening

1 cup sugar

¹/₄ cup molasses

1 egg

2¹/₄ cups flour

2 teaspoons baking soda

1 teaspoon cinnamon

¹/₂ teaspoon each cloves, ginger and salt

¹/₄ cup sugar

Yield: 12 to 18 cookies

- Cream the shortening and 1 cup sugar in a mixer bowl until light and fluffy. Stir in the molasses and egg.
- Mix the flour, baking soda, cinnamon, cloves, ginger and salt in a bowl. Add the molasses mixture; mix well. Shape into 1-inch balls. Pour ¹/₄ cup sugar onto a small plate. Roll the balls in the sugar. Place on a nonstick cookie sheet. Bake at 375 degrees for 8 to 10 minutes. Do not brown. Cool on a wire rack.

Tea Time Cookies

1 cup butter, softened
2 cups packed brown sugar
2 eggs
3½ cups flour
1 teaspoon baking soda
½ teaspoon salt
¾ cup finely chopped pecans

Yield: 24 cookies

- Cream the butter and brown sugar in a mixer bowl until light and fluffy. Beat in the eggs 1 at a time.
- Mix the flour, baking soda, salt and pecans together. Fold into the batter.
- Chill, covered with plastic wrap, in refrigerator overnight or for up to 2 weeks.
- Roll the chilled dough very thin on a lightly floured surface. Cut with a cookie cutter; place on a lightly greased cookie sheet.
- Bake at 375 degrees for 10 to 15 minutes or until golden brown. Cool on a wire rack.

Shortbread Cookies

2 cups butter, softened
1 cup sugar
1 teaspoon almond extract
4 cups flour
5 cups roasted almonds

Yield: 24 cookies

- Cream the butter and sugar in a mixer bowl until light and fluffy. Add the almond flavoring, flour and almonds; mix well.
- Pat the dough into a 7x10-inch rectangle, ⅜ inch thick on a nonstick cookie sheet.
- Cut lines in the dough, forming 1½-inch squares. Chill in refrigerator.
- Bake at 275 degrees for 40 minutes or until light brown. Cool on a wire rack.
- Break into cookies along the cut lines.

Speculaasjes Koekjes*
(Santa Claus Cookies)

2 cups sugar

2 cups butter, softened

4 cups flour, sifted

4 teaspoons cinnamon

1/2 teaspoon each nutmeg, cloves and
   baking soda

1/4 teaspoon salt

1/2 cup each sour cream and almonds

Yield: 60 cookies

- Cream the sugar and butter in a mixer bowl until light and fluffy. Sift the flour, cinnamon, nutmeg, cloves, baking soda and salt together. Add to the creamed mixture alternately with sour cream, beating constantly.
- Chop the almonds. Stir into the creamed mixture; knead well. Shape the dough into a loaf; wrap in waxed paper and chill overnight. Cut the dough into slices; place on a greased cookie sheet.
- Bake at 400 degrees until light brown. Cool.

Kruimel Koek*
(Dutch Crumb Cake)

2 1/2 cups flour

1/2 teaspoon salt

1/2 teaspoon baking soda

1/2 cup shortening

3/4 cup packed brown sugar

1 cup raisins, ground

1 egg, beaten

3/4 cup thick sour milk

2 tablespoons sugar

1/8 teaspoon cinnamon

Yield: 9 servings

- Sift the flour, salt and baking soda together. Beat the shortening in a mixer bowl until creamy. Add the brown sugar gradually, beating until light and fluffy. Add the flour mixture; mix well. Reserve 3/4 cup of the mixture; set aside.
- Combine the ground raisins, egg and sour milk in a bowl; mix well. Add to the flour mixture; mix well. Spoon into a greased 8x8-inch cake pan. Sprinkle the reserved mixture over the top. Sprinkle a mixture of the sugar and cinnamon over the top.
- Bake at 350 degrees for 25 minutes or until the cake tests done.

$\mathscr{P}$EPER $\mathscr{K}$OEK*

(Dutch Spice Cake)

1 cup packed brown sugar

1/2 cup shortening

2 eggs, beaten

1 teaspoon baking soda

1/2 cup molasses

1/2 cup cold water

2 cups flour

1 teaspoon ginger

1 teaspoon cinnamon

1/8 teaspoon salt

2 cups packed brown sugar

2 tablespoons flour

2 cups hot water

2 tablespoons butter

2 teaspoons vanilla extract

Yield: 12 servings

- Cream 1 cup brown sugar and shortening in a mixer bowl until light and fluffy.
- Add the eggs; beat well.
- Stir the baking soda into the molasses until dissolved; add to the creamed mixture.
- Add the cold water; mix well.
- Sift 2 cups flour, ginger, cinnamon and salt together.
- Add to the creamed mixture; mix well.
- Spoon into a greased 7x11-inch cake pan.
- Bake at 300 degrees for 40 minutes or until the cake tests done.
- Cool on a wire rack.
- Combine 2 cups brown sugar and 2 tablespoons flour in a saucepan.
- Stir in the hot water.
- Cook over medium heat until thickened, stirring constantly.
- Remove from the heat.
- Stir in the butter and vanilla.
- Serve hot over the cake.

⅂ROPISCHE ⅁EMBERKOEK*

(Tropical Gingerbread)

½ cup butter, softened

½ cup sugar

2 eggs, beaten

1 teaspoon baking soda

½ cup molasses

1 teaspoon ginger

1 teaspoon cinnamon

¼ teaspoon salt

1½ cups flour

½ cup cold water

1 cup flaked coconut

1 cup sugar

1 cup water

2 egg whites, at room temperature

1 teaspoon orange or lemon extract

1 cup flaked coconut

Yield: 15 servings

- Cream the butter and ½ cup sugar in a mixer bowl until light and fluffy.
- Add the eggs; mix well.
- Dissolve the baking soda in the molasses in a bowl.
- Add to the egg mixture.
- Sift the ginger, cinnamon, salt and flour together.
- Add to the batter alternately with ½ cup cold water, mixing well after each addition.
- Stir in 1 cup coconut.
- Spoon the batter into a greased 9x13-inch baking pan.
- Bake at 350 degrees for 30 to 35 minutes or until the gingerbread tests done.
- Cool in the pan on a wire rack.
- Combine the 1 cup sugar and 1 cup water in a saucepan.
- Cook over high heat until mixture is 230 to 235 degrees on a candy thermometer, spun-thread stage; do not stir.
- Beat the egg whites in a mixer bowl until soft peaks form.
- Add the boiling syrup very gradually, beating constantly.
- Add the orange flavoring.
- Fold in half the remaining coconut. Spread the frosting over the cooled gingerbread.
- Sprinkle the remaining coconut on top.

Nutmeg Cake

2 cups packed brown sugar
2 cups flour
1/2 cup shortening
1 egg
1 teaspoon nutmeg
1 cup sour cream
1 teaspoon baking soda
1/2 cup walnuts, chopped

Yield: 9 servings

- Mix the brown sugar and flour in a bowl.
- Cut in the shortening until the mixture is crumbly. Spoon half the mixture into a greased 9x9-inch cake pan.
- Add the egg to the remaining mixture; mix well.
- Add a mixture of the nutmeg, sour cream and baking soda; mix well.
- Spoon into the prepared pan. Sprinkle with the walnuts.
- Bake at 350 degrees for 40 to 45 minutes or until a wooden pick inserted near the center comes out clean.

Southern Pound Cake

1 1/2 cups butter, softened
1 2/3 cups sugar
5 eggs
2 cups sifted cake flour
1 teaspoon vanilla extract
2 tablespoons confectioners' sugar

Yield: 16 servings

- Beat the butter in a mixer bowl until soft. Add the sugar gradually, mixing well after each addition.
- Beat in the eggs 1 at a time. Beat in the flour 1/3 cup at a time, mixing well after each addition.
- Add the vanilla; mix well. Spoon the batter into a greased and floured tube pan.
- Bake at 325 degrees for 1 hour or until the cake tests done. Cool in the pan on a wire rack for 5 minutes.
- Remove to a serving plate to cool completely. Sprinkle with the confectioners' sugar.

$\mathscr{B}$ANKET*
(Almond Roll)

1 cup almond or macaroon paste
1 cup sugar
1 egg
1 egg yolk
¼ cup cornstarch
1 cup butter, softened
2 cups flour
¼ cup water
1 egg white, beaten

Yield: 48 servings

- Place the almond paste, sugar, egg, egg yolk and cornstarch in a bowl.
- Let stand at room temperature for 30 minutes.
- Cut the butter into the flour in a bowl until crumbly.
- Add the water a small amount at a time, mixing with a fork until the mixture forms a ball.
- Divide the dough into 2 equal portions.
- Roll each portion on a floured surface into an 8x13-inch rectangle.
- Cut lengthwise into 2 equal strips.
- Stir the almond paste mixture until well blended.
- Shape into four 12-inch long cylinders the diameter of a dime.
- Place each cylinder on 1 strip of dough.
- Fold up each end; fold the long sides to enclose the filling, moistening one side and pressing to seal.
- Place seam side down on a nonstick cookie sheet.
- Pierce holes on top to vent.
- Brush the tops of the rolls with the beaten egg white.
- Bake at 400 degrees for 14 minutes. Reduce oven temperature to 325 degrees.
- Bake for 20 minutes longer or until light brown. Cool on a wire rack. Slice into 1-inch pieces.
- Dough may be prepared ahead and refrigerated overnight if desired.

After-School Treats

Sip your tea, while they sip their milk—enjoy.

2 cups creamy peanut butter
1/2 cup melted butter
1 (1-pound) package confectioners' sugar
3 cups crisp rice cereal
1 package chocolate almond bark

Yield: 60 treats

- Combine the peanut butter and butter in a bowl; mix well.
- Stir in the confectioners' sugar and rice cereal.
- Shape by teaspoonfuls into balls. Place on a tray. Chill in the refrigerator.
- Melt the chocolate almond bark in a saucepan over low heat, stirring frequently.
- Dip chilled treats into chocolate until coated; drain. Place on waxed paper. Let stand until set.

Christmas English Toffee

1 cup sugar
3 tablespoons water
1 cup butter
1 teaspoon vanilla extract
1 cup bittersweet chocolate chips or broken chocolate bar
1/2 to 1 cup chopped pecans or other nuts

Yield: 20 servings

- Combine the sugar, water and butter in a saucepan.
- Cook over medium-high heat for 10 minutes or until mixture turns dark tan in color, stirring constantly.
- Stir in the vanilla.
- Pour onto a buttered baking sheet or buttered marble slab.
- Sprinkle the chocolate chips over the top, spreading as they melt.
- Sprinkle with the pecans. Let stand overnight until cool and firm. Break into bite-size pieces.

GEBRUIKEN

To Partake of Food and Drink

DUTCH KLOMPEN DANCERS:
TRADITIONAL WOODEN SHOE DANCE DURING TULIP TIME FESTIVAL

Holland Camera Club

$\mathscr{G}$EBRUIKEN

*Most requested recipe from **Eet Smakelijk**

Chicken Satay

8 chicken breasts
¼ cup soy sauce
1 tablespoon vegetable oil
1 tablespoon molasses
¼ teaspoon white or red pepper
1 clove of garlic, minced
3 tablespoons lemon juice
½ cup peanut butter
½ cup hot water

Yield: 8 servings

- Rinse the chicken; pat dry.
- Pound the chicken with a meat mallet to ½-inch thickness.
- Cut into strips.
- Place in a shallow glass bowl.
- Mix the soy sauce, oil, molasses, pepper, garlic and 1 tablespoon lemon juice in a bowl.
- Pour over the chicken.
- Marinate, covered, in refrigerator for 2 hours.
- Soak bamboo skewers for 20 minutes in water to cover in a bowl; drain.
- Drain the chicken, reserving marinade.
- Thread the chicken onto skewers; place on a rack in broiler pan.
- Brush the chicken with reserved marinade.
- Broil for 4 to 5 minutes.
- Turn chicken; brush with marinade.
- Broil for 2 to 3 minutes longer or until cooked through.
- Do not overcook. Leave chicken on skewers and place on serving dish.
- Combine the remaining 2 tablespoons lemon juice, peanut butter and hot water in a bowl; mix until smooth.
- Serve with the hot chicken.

Antipasto Kabobs

A neat way to serve antipasto.

12 ounces large mushrooms, cleaned and stems removed

1 (8-ounce) can artichoke hearts, drained

1 (6-ounce) can whole black olives

2 cups cherry tomatoes

2 red bell peppers, roasted, coarsely chopped

1½ cups tarragon vinegar

1½ cups olive oil

1 large onion, finely chopped

5 cloves of garlic, minced

2 teaspoons sugar

1 tablespoon basil

1 tablespoon oregano

1 tablespoon black pepper

Yield: 16 servings

- Cut the mushrooms and artichoke hearts into quarters.
- Combine the mushrooms, artichoke hearts, black olives, cherry tomatoes and red bell peppers in a 9x13-inch glass dish.
- Combine the vinegar, olive oil, onion, garlic, sugar, basil, oregano and black pepper in a saucepan.
- Bring to a boil over medium heat; reduce heat.
- Simmer for 5 minutes, stirring occasionally.
- Pour over the vegetables, tossing to coat.
- Marinate, covered, in the refrigerator for 12 hours or longer, tossing to coat occasionally.
- Drain vegetables up to 2 hours before serving time.
- Arrange 1 of each kind of vegetable on 4-inch skewers; place on serving platter.
- Chill, covered, in refrigerator.
- Serve with hard salami and a variety of cheeses and breads.

Tortellini Kabobs

An appetizer with an Italian flavor.

8 ounces cheese-filled tortellini, cooked
8 ounces sliced salami, cut into halves
5 ounces green olives
1/2 cup Italian salad dressing

Yield: 36 kabobs

- Combine the tortellini, salami, green olives and salad dressing in a shallow dish; stirring gently to coat.
- Chill, covered, for 4 to 6 hours, stirring occasionally; drain.
- Thread the tortellini, salami and green olives onto thirty-six 4-inch skewers, folding the salami in half before threading.

Fruited Chicken Wings

A new way to serve a favorite munchie.

2 1/2 pounds chicken wings
4 ounces apricot jam
1/2 teaspoon garlic powder
1 teaspoon dry mustard
5 ounces soy sauce

Yield: 10 servings

- Rinse chicken; pat dry.
- Disjoin chicken wings, discarding tips. Place in a shallow dish.
- Combine the apricot jam, garlic powder, mustard and soy sauce in a bowl; mix well.
- Pour over the chicken.
- Marinate, covered, in refrigerator overnight.
- Drain the chicken, reserving marinade. Place the chicken on a foil-lined baking sheet.
- Bake at 350 degrees for 1 hour or until cooked through, basting with reserved marinade several times.

Almond Fried Shrimp

Serve with marmalade for dipping.

1 large egg
1 cup skim milk
½ teaspoon salt
1 cup flour
18 saltine crackers, finely crushed
½ cup finely chopped blanched almonds
2 tablespoons chopped chives or green onions
1 pound peeled shrimp
Vegetable oil for frying

Yield: 28 servings

- Whisk the egg, milk and salt in a bowl.
- Place flour in a second bowl. Combine cracker crumbs, almonds and chives in a third bowl.
- Dip shrimp 1 at a time into egg mixture to coat; dredge in flour. Dip in egg mixture again; roll in cracker mixture to coat. Place in a single layer on a flat surface.
- Heat 1½ inches of oil in a deep skillet to 375 degrees. Fry shrimp several at a time for 30 to 40 seconds on each side or until golden brown. Drain on paper towels.

Crab Rangoon

4 ounces crab meat, chopped
4 ounces cream cheese, softened
¼ teaspoon steak sauce
⅛ teaspoon garlic powder
Won ton wrappers
1 egg yolk, beaten
Vegetable oil for deep-frying

Yield: 8 servings

- Combine the crab meat, cream cheese, steak sauce and garlic powder in a bowl; mix well.
- Place ½ teaspoon crab meat mixture in the center of each won ton wrapper.
- Bring corners up to center, forming a pouch. Brush with egg yolk; press to seal.
- Drop several at a time into hot oil.
- Deep-fry until light brown. Remove with a slotted spoon; drain on paper towels.

ROQUEFORT GRAPES

Unique and elegant.

1 (10-ounce) package walnuts, pecans, almonds or macadamia nuts

8 ounces cream cheese, softened

4 ounces Roquefort cheese

2 tablespoons whipping cream

1 pound seedless red or green grapes

Yield: 10 servings

- Place the walnuts on a baking sheet. Bake at 275 degrees for 10 minutes or until walnuts are toasted. Chop coarsely; spread on a flat surface.
- Combine the cream cheese, Roquefort cheese and whipping cream in a bowl. Beat until mixture is blended.
- Rinse the grapes; pat dry with paper towels. Drop grapes several at a time into cheese mixture, stirring gently to coat.
- Roll the grapes in chopped walnuts; place on a waxed-paper lined tray. Chill until serving time.
- Arrange on a large serving platter in the shape of a bunch of grapes. Garnish with grape leaves or vines.

ASPARAGUS ROLL-UPS

Easy and luxurious.

1 loaf Pepperidge Farm thin-sliced white bread

8 ounces cream cheese, softened

4 ounces bleu cheese, grated or chopped

1 egg

1 bunch fresh asparagus, ends removed

Yield: 12 servings

- Remove crusts from bread slices. Combine the cream cheese, bleu cheese and egg in a bowl; mix well.
- Spread on 1 side of each slice of bread.
- Place 1 piece of asparagus over cheese mixture; roll up bread to enclose. Place seam-side down on a nonstick baking sheet.
- Bake at 400 degrees for 12 minutes.

GEBRUIKEN

Gouda Bread Appetizer

This can be prepared ahead and baked just before serving. Great with crackers and fresh fruit.

1 (8-count) can crescent dinner rolls

2 tablespoons Dijon mustard, or to taste

1 (8-ounce) package Gouda cheese

1 egg white, slightly beaten

1 tablespoon sesame seeds

Yield: 12 servings

- Unroll crescent roll dough on a nonstick baking pan, pressing perforations to seal.
- Brush with mustard.
- Place the Gouda cheese in center of the dough.
- Fold up the long edges of dough to enclose the cheese, pressing edges together to seal.
- Brush with egg white; sprinkle with sesame seeds.
- Bake at 350 degrees for 20 minutes or until golden brown.

Herb Bread

This tasty treat will disappear quickly.

1/2 cup butter, softened

1 teaspoon parsley

1/4 teaspoon oregano

1/4 teaspoon dillweed

1/4 teaspoon garlic powder

2 tablespoons grated Parmesan cheese

1 loaf French bread, split lengthwise

Yield: 30 servings

- Combine the butter, parsley, oregano, dillweed, garlic powder and Parmesan cheese in a bowl; mix well.
- Spread on the cut side of the French bread.
- Place the bread on a nonstick baking sheet.
- Bake at 400 degrees for 10 minutes.

Focaccia

This versatile appetizer may be served hot or cold.

1 package, or 1 recipe pizza dough
Olive oil
Sliced tomatoes
Oregano to taste
Basil to taste
Minced garlic to taste
Grated Parmesan cheese
Salt and pepper to taste

Yield: 8 servings

- Prepare the pizza dough and let rise using package directions.
- Spread the dough on a large greased baking sheet.
- Brush the olive oil over dough.
- Arrange the tomato slices on dough; sprinkle with the oregano, basil, garlic, Parmesan cheese, salt and pepper.
- Bake at 350 degrees for 20 minutes or until the edges are brown.
- Cut into servings.

Pepperoni Bread

1 loaf frozen bread dough
1 egg, beaten
8 ounces sliced pepperoni
8 ounces shredded mozzarella cheese
1 teaspoon oregano
1 tablespoon grated Parmesan cheese
Melted butter

Yield: 8 servings

- Thaw the frozen bread dough using package directions.
- Roll the dough as thin and round as possible on a lightly floured surface.
- Brush the dough with beaten egg.
- Layer the pepperoni, mozzarella cheese, oregano and Parmesan cheese over the dough.
- Roll up the dough into a tight roll, enclosing the filling. Place seam-side down on a baking sheet. Brush with melted butter.
- Bake at 350 degrees for 30 to 35 minutes or until brown.

Tomato and Fennel Spread on Bruschetta

This is great when you are asked to bring an appetizer.

2 tomatoes, seeded, finely chopped

½ fennel bulb, trimmed, finely chopped

½ cup olive oil

¼ cup chopped fresh basil

Salt and pepper to taste

1 bruschetta baguette

Garlic

Yield: 12 servings

- Combine chopped tomatoes, fennel bulb, ½ cup olive oil, ¼ cup basil, salt and pepper in a bowl; mix well.
- Cut bruschetta into slices.
- Spread additional olive oil and garlic on each slice.
- Toast bruschetta lightly.
- Spoon the tomato mixture onto each bruschetta slice.
- Serve warm.

Toasted Parmesan Canapes

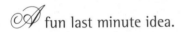 fun last minute idea.

3 tablespoons grated Parmesan cheese

1 cup mayonnaise

3 tablespoons finely chopped onion

16 (1½-inch diameter) rounds of sliced white bread

Grated Parmesan cheese

Yield: 16 servings

- Mix the 3 tablespoons Parmesan cheese, mayonnaise and onion together in a bowl.
- Spread the cheese mixture on 1 side of each bread round; sprinkle with additional Parmesan cheese.
- Place on rack in broiler pan.
- Toast under hot broiler until brown.
- Serve immediately.

Greek Spinach Pie

*G*reat way to serve spinach as an appetizer or side dish.

1 package frozen phyllo dough
1 pound fresh spinach
3 tablespoons olive oil
1 1/4 cups finely chopped onions
3/4 cup chopped green onions
1/2 cup butter or margarine
4 eggs, beaten
1 1/2 pounds feta cheese, crumbled
1 tablespoon dried dill
1/2 cup chopped parsley
Pepper to taste
Melted unsalted butter

Yield: 6 servings

- Thaw phyllo dough at room temperature.
- Do not unwrap until ready to use.
- Rinse the spinach; pat dry. Cut or tear into 1- to 2-inch pieces.
- Cook the spinach in olive oil in a large skillet just until wilted, stirring frequently; drain.
- Sauté the onions and green onions in 1/2 cup butter in a skillet.
- Combine the sautéed onions, eggs, cheese, dill and parsley in a large bowl; mix well. Stir in the spinach and pepper.
- Butter an 8x8-inch baking pan. Cut the phyllo dough into squares to fit the baking pan.
- Place 2 squares of phyllo dough in the baking pan; brush top with butter. Repeat procedure 5 times.
- Spread 1/2 of the spinach mixture over layers.
- Place 2 squares of phyllo dough over spinach mixture; brush top with butter. Repeat procedure 5 times.
- Add remaining spinach mixture. Top with 2 squares of phyllo dough; brush top with butter. Repeat procedure 5 times.
- Cut through top layer of phyllo dough, scoring the dough into 12 squares.
- Bake at 400 degrees for 1 hour or until golden brown and puffy. Cool for 10 minutes. Cut into 12 squares.
- Serve hot or cold.

Susan Bartolomei's Pesto and Salmon Torta

Award winning area cook and culinary student contributed this crowd-pleaser.

36 ounces cream cheese, softened
1 cup unsalted butter, softened
1 (7-ounce) package pesto
6 ounces smoked salmon, finely chopped
1 (4-ounce) can chopped black olives, drained
Chopped pistachio nuts

Yield: 12 servings

- Beat 24 ounces of the cream cheese and butter in a large mixer bowl until smooth.
- Combine 4 ounces of the cream cheese and pesto in a bowl; mix well.
- Combine 4 ounces of the cream cheese and salmon in a bowl; mix well.
- Combine the remaining 4 ounces of cream cheese and olives in a bowl; mix well.
- Line a 5x9-inch loaf pan with plastic wrap, overlapping edges generously.
- Divide the butter mixture into 4 equal portions (about 1 cup each).
- Layer 1 portion of the butter mixture, pesto mixture, 1 portion of the butter mixture, salmon mixture, 1 portion of the butter mixture, olive mixture and remaining butter mixture in prepared pan.
- Fold plastic wrap over top to cover torta, pressing firmly to compact.
- Chill in refrigerator for 6 hours to 3 days.
- Remove plastic wrap from top; invert onto serving platter, removing remaining plastic wrap.
- Press pistachio nuts over top and sides.

Herbed Cheesecake

16 ounces cream cheese, softened

1/2 cup Dijon mustard

1/2 cup whipping cream

4 eggs

1/2 cup chopped onion

1 tablespoon each fresh basil, thyme, rosemary and chives

Salt to taste

Dash of Tabasco sauce

1/4 cup lightly toasted bread crumbs

Yield: 20 servings

- Process the cream cheese, mustard, cream, eggs, onion, basil, thyme, rosemary, chives, salt and Tabasco sauce in a food processor until smooth.
- Spray an 8- or 9-inch springform pan with nonstick cooking spray; coat with bread crumbs.
- Spoon the cream cheese mixture into prepared pan.
- Bake at 350 degrees for 50 minutes or until cheesecake is set.
- Place pan on a wire rack; cool completely.
- Place on a serving plate; remove side of springform pan. Chill cheesecake in refrigerator.
- Serve with crackers.

Onalee's Pickles

They'll never know you didn't start with garden cucumbers.

1 (20-ounce) jar whole dill pickles

1/2 cup vinegar

1/2 cup water

2 cups sugar

1 1/2 tablespoons mixed pickling spices

Yield: 20 servings

- Drain the pickles; cover with boiling water.
- Let stand overnight; drain.
- Slice pickles lengthwise and return to jar.
- Combine the vinegar, water, sugar and pickling spices in a saucepan. Bring to a boil.
- Cook over medium heat for 5 minutes, stirring frequently. Pour over pickles. Store, covered, in refrigerator.

Baked Garlic with Sun-Dried Tomatoes

An unusual twist to traditional baked garlic.

4 large heads garlic
2¹/₂ tablespoons butter, thinly sliced
¹/₄ cup olive oil
2 cups chicken broth
2 cups sun-dried tomatoes
1 tablespoon dried basil
1 tablespoon dried oregano
Pepper to taste
6 ounces goat cheese, sliced
Fresh basil leaves
1 loaf Italian bread, sliced

Yield: 16 servings

- Cut ¹/₄-inch slice from top of garlic heads; discard. Remove any loose papery peeling. Place the garlic cut-side up in a medium baking dish. Arrange butter slices over garlic; pour olive oil over garlic. Pour chicken broth around garlic; arrange sun-dried tomatoes in broth. Sprinkle with basil, oregano and pepper.

- Bake at 375 degrees for 1 hour and 15 minutes or until garlic and tomatoes are tender, basting with broth every 15 minutes. Arrange goat cheese around garlic.

- Bake for 10 minutes longer or until goat cheese is almost melted. Garnish with fresh basil. Serve with Italian bread slices.

Brown Sugar and Nut-Glazed Brie

Rich and sweet.

¹/₄ cup packed brown sugar
1 tablespoon bourbon whiskey
¹/₄ cup chopped pecans
1 (14-ounce) wheel of Brie cheese

Yield: 10 servings

- Combine the brown sugar, whiskey and pecans in a microwave-safe dish. Microwave on High until brown sugar dissolves; mix well.

- Place the Brie cheese in a microwave-safe serving dish. Pour hot brown sugar mixture over cheese.

- Microwave on High for 2 to 3 minutes or until heated through. Serve with crackers.

Clearbrook's Gratin of Woodland Mushrooms

Clearbrook Restaurant, located in Saugatuck, overlooks Clearbrook's premier golf course. Luke Finchem, Executive Chef, contributed this delicacy.

4 to 6 frozen puff pastry shells

2 cups whipping cream

4 to 6 cloves of garlic, peeled

1 tablespoon vegetable oil

2 tablespoons butter

4 cups sliced assorted mushrooms such as shiitake, creminis, portobellos, button, oyster

1 tablespoon chopped fresh herbs such as basil, thyme, rosemary

Salt and pepper to taste

1 cup grated fontina cheese or Swiss cheese

2 tablespoons grated Parmesan cheese

Yield: 4 to 6 servings

- Bake the puff pastry shells using package directions.
- Pour the cream into a heavy saucepan. Boil over medium heat for 10 to 15 minutes or until reduced, stirring frequently.
- Place the peeled garlic in a roasting pan with the oil.
- Bake at 375 degrees until golden brown. Drain the oil into a skillet. Add the garlic to the cream. Simmer the cream for 10 minutes longer, stirring occasionally. Remove from heat.
- Add the butter to the oil in the skillet. Heat until very hot. Add the mushrooms.
- Sauté until the mushrooms are soft but still hold their shape. Remove from heat. Stir in the herbs, salt and pepper.
- Place the puff pastry shells on a rack in a broiler pan.
- Spoon the mushrooms into the puff pastry shells; add 3 to 4 tablespoons of the garlic cream to each. Sprinkle with the fontina cheese; top with the Parmesan cheese.
- Broil under a hot broiler until the cheese melts. Serve immediately.
- *Note:* May cook the mushrooms and prepare the garlic cream up to 3 days before using. Store in the refrigerator. Bake the puff pastry shells the day they are to be used. May also bake the appetizers at 425 degrees until the cheese melts.

Chevre Pine Nut Toasts with Sun-Dried Tomato Pesto

You'll earn a gourmet reputation with this easy recipe.

8 ounces cream cheese, softened

4 ounces goat cheese (chèvre), crumbled

1 tablespoon vodka

4 cloves of garlic, minced

3 tablespoons olive oil

1 (14-ounce) can Italian plum tomatoes, coarsely chopped

1/2 cup sun-dried tomato halves in oil

1/4 cup shredded fresh basil

1 French bread baguette

1/4 cup toasted pine nuts

Yield: 20 servings

- Process the cream cheese, goat cheese and vodka in a food processor until smooth.
- Chill, covered, until serving time.
- Sauté the garlic in olive oil in a large skillet just until heated through; do not brown.
- Add the Italian tomatoes.
- Simmer over medium-low heat for 1 hour or until thickened, stirring frequently.
- Drain the sun-dried tomatoes, reserving the oil.
- Chop enough sun-dried tomatoes to measure 1/2 cup.
- Stir into the Italian tomato mixture; cool slightly.
- Process in a food processor until puréed.
- Add reserved oil and basil.
- Process until blended.
- Chill pesto, covered, until serving time.
- Cut the bread diagonally into slices.
- Place on a rack in a broiler pan.
- Toast under hot broiler until light brown on each side.
- Spread cheese mixture on each bread slice; sprinkle with pine nuts.
- Place 1 teaspoon of tomato pesto in center of each.

Baked Goat Cheese

Easy and elegant.

1 package goat cheese
1¹/₂ cups tomato-basil spaghetti sauce
Minced garlic to taste
Chopped basil to taste
Cracked black pepper to taste
Chopped oregano to taste
1 loaf French bread
Butter or margarine, softened

Yield: 16 servings

- Place goat cheese in a small baking dish.
- Pour 1¹/₂ cups spaghetti sauce over cheese.
- Sprinkle with the garlic, basil and cracked black pepper.
- Bake at 350 degrees for 30 minutes or until the cheese is heated through.
- Cut the French bread diagonally into slices.
- Spread butter on one side of bread; sprinkle with garlic, basil, oregano and pepper.
- Toast the garlic bread.
- Place the goat cheese on a serving plate surrounded by the garlic toast.

Cheese Fondue

A quick easy way to make your guests feel special.

1 cup French onion dip
1 (10-ounce) can Cheddar cheese soup
4 ounces Cheddar cheese, shredded
¹/₂ teaspoon dry mustard
¹/₄ teaspoon red pepper
French bread cubes

Yield: 30 servings

- Combine the onion dip, cheese soup, cheese, mustard and pepper in a saucepan.
- Heat over medium heat until the cheese is melted and the mixture is smooth, stirring constantly.
- Spoon into a chafing dish. Serve with bread cubes.

Pesto Cream Cheese Spread

If you like pesto, you'll love this.

1 tablespoon melted butter

¹/₄ cup fine cracker crumbs

12 ounces cream cheese, softened

2 eggs

¹/₄ cup whipping cream

2 tablespoons melted butter

2 cups shredded Parmesan cheese

³/₄ cup pesto

¹/₄ cup toasted pine nuts

Fresh basil

Yield: 50 servings

- Brush 1 tablespoon melted butter on the inside of a baking dish; coat with the cracker crumbs. Beat the cream cheese in a mixer bowl until smooth. Beat in the eggs, cream and 2 tablespoons melted butter. Fold in the Parmesan cheese. Spoon into the prepared baking dish. Pour the pesto over the top, swirling into mixture with a spatula until lightly blended.
- Bake at 325 degrees for 45 minutes or until puffy and brown. Cool. Chill for 8 hours to 3 days. Bring to room temperature before serving. Sprinkle with pine nuts and basil leaves. Serve with assorted crackers.

Clam Bread

Your guests will rave about this recipe.

2 (6¹/₂-ounce) cans chopped or minced clams

16 ounces cream cheese, softened

6 green onions, chopped

6 tablespoons fresh parsley

¹/₂ teaspoon seasoned salt

1 round loaf bread

Yield: 30 servings

- Drain the clams, reserving ¹/₄ cup liquid. Combine the clams, reserved liquid, cream cheese, green onions, parsley and seasoned salt in a bowl; mix well.
- Cut and remove the center from the bread, leaving a ¹/₂-inch shell. Spoon the clam mixture into the bread shell. Wrap in foil; place on a baking sheet.
- Bake at 225 degrees for 3 hours. Cut the center removed from the bread into serving-size pieces. Serve with Clam Bread for dipping.

Hot Crab Meat Dip

*B*ake in a thick-sided stoneware casserole and it will stay warm a long time.

8 ounces cream cheese, softened
2 tablespoons chopped green onions
1/2 teaspoon prepared horseradish
1 (8-ounce) can crab meat
Dash of pepper
1 teaspoon Tabasco sauce

Yield: 12 servings

- Combine the cream cheese, green onions, horse-radish, crab meat, pepper and Tabasco sauce in a bowl; mix well.
- Spoon into a buttered casserole.
- Bake, uncovered, at 375 degrees for 15 to 20 minutes or until heated through.
- Serve with crackers or bread.

Crunchy Cheese Ball

A tailgater's delight.

8 ounces cream cheese, softened
¼ cup mayonnaise
2 cups finely chopped cooked ham
2 tablespoons chopped parsley
1 teaspoon minced onion
¼ teaspoon dry mustard
¼ teaspoon hot pepper sauce
½ cup chopped peanuts

Yield: 24 servings

- Combine the cream cheese and mayonnaise in a bowl; mix well.
- Stir in the ham, parsley, onion, mustard and hot pepper sauce.
- Chill, covered, for several hours.
- Shape into a ball; roll in the chopped peanuts.

Thanksgiving Day Cheese Ball

A great snack to enjoy while the turkey is cooking.

8 ounces cream cheese, softened
¼ cup butter or margarine, softened
1 cup black olives, chopped
8 ounces bleu cheese, crumbled
1 teaspoon lemon juice
1 tablespoon finely chopped green
   onions
Chopped pecans

Yield: 48 servings

- Combine the cream cheese, butter, olives, bleu cheese, lemon juice and green onions in a bowl; mix well.
- Shape into a ball. Roll in the chopped pecans to coat.
- Chill, covered, until serving time.

Apple Dip

8 ounces cream cheese, softened
³⁄₄ cup packed brown sugar
¹⁄₄ cup sugar
1 teaspoon vanilla extract
1 cup peanuts, chopped

Yield: 30 servings

- Combine the cream cheese, brown sugar, sugar, vanilla and peanuts in a bowl; mix well.
- Spoon into a serving dish. Serve with apple wedges.

Harvest Dip

Always a hit.

16 ounces cream cheese, softened
1 (4-ounce) can juice-pack crushed pineapple
¹⁄₂ cup chopped pecans
¹⁄₄ cup chopped onion
¹⁄₄ cup chopped green bell pepper

Yield: 16 servings

- Combine the cream cheese and undrained pineapple in a bowl; mix well.
- Add the pecans, onion and green pepper; mix well.
- Chill, covered, until serving time.
- Serve with crackers.

Feta Cheese Dip

Keep in your refrigerator during the holidays to serve unexpected guests.

4 ounces feta cheese, crumbled

8 ounces plain yogurt

1 clove of garlic, minced

1/4 cup fresh parsley, finely chopped

1 tablespoon dillweed or 2 tablespoons
  chopped fresh dill

Juice of 1 lemon

Pinch of cayenne

Yield: 20 servings

- Combine the feta cheese and yogurt in a bowl;
  mix well.
- Add the garlic, parsley, dillweed, lemon juice and
  cayenne; mix well.
- Chill for several hours to overnight before serving.
- Serve with pita chips, breadsticks or crisp vegetables.

Hot and Spicy Bean Dip

A football fan favorite.

8 ounces cream cheese, softened

1 (10-ounce) can bean dip

20 drops of hot pepper sauce

1 to 2 teaspoons chili powder

Salt to taste

1 cup sour cream

1/2 cup sliced green onions

1/2 envelope taco seasoning mix

4 ounces Cheddar cheese, shredded

4 ounces Monterey Jack cheese,
  shredded

Yield: 20 servings

- Mix the cream cheese, bean dip, hot pepper sauce,
  chili powder, salt, sour cream, green onions and taco
  seasoning mix in a mixer bowl.
- Layer cream cheese mixture, Cheddar cheese and
  Monterey Jack cheese 1/2 at a time in 1 1/2-quart baking
  dish or chafing dish.
- Bake at 350 degrees for 20 minutes or until heated
  through.
- Serve warm with tortilla chips.
- May make ahead and freeze until time to bake. Allow
  extra time for baking if frozen.

Fresh Picante

This also tastes great served on top of taco salad.

3 medium tomatoes, seeded, chopped
1 green bell pepper, chopped
1/2 cup chopped onion or green onions
1 Anaheim chile pepper, finely chopped
2 tablespoons chopped fresh cilantro
2 cloves of garlic, minced
1 tablespoon lime or lemon juice
  concentrate
1/2 teaspoon each chili powder and cumin
1/2 teaspoon garlic salt

Yield: 4 cups

- Combine the tomatoes, bell pepper, onion, chile pepper, cilantro, garlic, lime juice, chili powder, cumin and garlic salt in a bowl; mix well.
- Chill, covered, in refrigerator.
- Serve with tortilla chips.

Mom's Salsa

If you want an extra hot salsa leave the seeds in some of the peppers.

8 cups crushed peeled tomatoes
8 to 10 peppers (mixture of bell,
  banana and jalapeño), chopped
3 medium onions, chopped
1/2 cup vinegar
1 (12-ounce) can tomato paste
1 tablespoon minced garlic
1 tablespoon black pepper
1 tablespoon salt

Yield: 80 servings

- Combine the tomatoes, peppers, onions, vinegar, tomato paste, garlic, black pepper and salt in a large saucepan. Bring to a boil, stirring occasionally. Simmer over low heat for 1 1/2 hours, stirring occasionally.
- Ladle into hot sterilized jars, leaving 1/2 inch headspace; seal with 2-piece lids.
- Process in a boiling water bath for 10 minutes.
- May also be stored in refrigerator.

Summer Slush

Refreshing summertime drink.

7 cups boiling water

1½ cups sugar

2 cups boiling water

4 tea bags

1 (12-ounce) can frozen orange juice
concentrate, thawed

1 (12-ounce) can frozen lemonade
concentrate, thawed

2 cups apricot brandy

12 cans lemon-lime soda

Yield: 20 servings

- Pour 7 cups of boiling water over the sugar in a large freezer container, stirring until the sugar dissolves.
- Pour 2 cups of boiling water over the tea bags in a bowl.
- Let steep for 5 minutes; remove tea bags.
- Add tea to sugar mixture.
- Cool to room temperature.
- Stir in orange juice concentrate, lemonade concentrate and brandy.
- Freeze, covered, overnight.
- Fill a glass ¾ full of frozen slush; add enough lemon-lime soda to fill the glass.

Strawberry Refresher

1 (10-ounce) package frozen
sweetened strawberries

1 (6-ounce) can frozen lemonade
concentrate, thawed

1 (8-ounce) can juice-pack crushed
pineapple

3 quarts ginger ale

Yield: 1 gallon

- Process the strawberries, lemonade concentrate and undrained crushed pineapple in a blender until puréed.
- Pour into a punch bowl or large pitcher.
- Add the ginger ale.

Let's Party Punch

2 (6-ounce) cans frozen lemonade
  concentrate, thawed
1 (6-ounce) can frozen orange juice
  concentrate, thawed
³/₄ cup lemon juice
1 fifth bourbon
2 liters lemon-lime soda

Yield: 20 servings

- Combine the lemonade concentrate, orange juice concentrate, lemon juice, bourbon and lemon-lime soda in a large freezer container; mix well.
- Freeze, covered, for 8 hours or longer.
- Remove from freezer 30 minutes before serving.
- Place in a punch bowl, stirring until slushy.

Susan Bartolomei's
Spiced Cranberry Apple Glogg

A wonderful creation from an area award-winning cooking instructor.

8 cups cranberry-apple juice cocktail
7 cups dry red wine
¹/₂ cup sugar
2 cinnamon sticks
8 whole cloves
Strips of orange peel or slices of star
  fruit

Yield: 8 servings

- Combine cranberry-apple juice cocktail, red wine, sugar, cinnamon sticks and cloves in a large saucepan.
- Heat over low heat to just below the simmering point.
- Heat for 1 hour, stirring occasionally.
- Ladle into mugs. Garnish with orange peel or star fruit.

BOERENJONGENS COCKTAIL*

Served especially during the Christmas season in Dutch homes.

1 pound raisins
2 cups water
1 cinnamon stick
2 cups sugar
2 cups whiskey or brandy

Yield: 1³/₄ quarts
- Combine the raisins, water and cinnamon stick in a saucepan.
- Cook over medium heat for 20 minutes, stirring frequently.
- Stir in the sugar and whiskey.
- Cook until the sugar dissolves, stirring constantly.
- Ladle into hot sterilized jars, leaving ¹/₂ inch headspace; seal. Let stand for 3 months.

BOERENMEISJES COCKTAIL*

This cocktail, being sweeter than the boerenjongens cocktail, is often served to the Dutch women while the men drink boerenjongens.

12 ounces dried apricots
Lemon peel
2 cups water
3 cups sugar
3 cups whiskey or brandy

Yield: 2 quarts
- Rinse the apricots.
- Place the apricots, lemon peel and water in a saucepan.
- Let stand for 24 hours.
- Cook over medium heat for 20 minutes or until the apricots are soft, stirring frequently. Add the sugar and whiskey, stirring until the sugar is dissolved.
- Ladle into hot sterilized jars, leaving ¹/₂ inch headspace; seal. Let stand for 3 months.

Into The Night

The Castle at Castle Park

A good day for a cup of hot chocolate.

Mary McDonald Theisen

Into the Night

*Most requested recipe from **Eet Smakelijk**

Fall Apple Pear Salad

Prepare in advance so salad may be chilled before serving. Nice accompaniment to pork.

1 cup cubed, unpeeled Red Delicious
  apple
1 cup cubed, unpeeled pear
1 cup red seedless grape halves
1 teaspoon lemon juice
1/4 cup mayonnaise
2 tablespoons honey
1/8 teaspoon cinnamon

Yield: 4 to 6 servings

- Combine the apple, pear and grapes in a bowl.
- Add the lemon juice; toss gently to coat.
- Combine the mayonnaise, honey and cinnamon in a bowl; mix well.
- Pour over the salad; toss gently to mix.
- Chill in the refrigerator. Serve on a bed of lettuce.

Lime Party Salad

16 large marshmallows
1 cup milk
1 (3-ounce) package lime gelatin
6 ounces cream cheese, softened
1 (8-ounce) can crushed pineapple
1 cup whipping cream, whipped

Yield: 8 servings

- Combine the marshmallows and milk in a saucepan.
- Cook over low heat until the marshmallows are melted, stirring frequently.
- Stir in the lime gelatin until dissolved.
- Add the cream cheese, stirring until dissolved.
- Remove from heat.
- Add the undrained crushed pineapple; mix well.
- Chill until partially set.
- Add the whipped cream, stirring gently to mix.
- Pour into a serving bowl or gelatin mold.
- Chill until set.

White Gelatin Salad

1 package unflavored gelatin
¼ cup cold water
1 cup boiling water
⅔ cup sugar
1 teaspoon vanilla extract
2 cups sour cream
8 ounces whipped topping
Strawberry Topping

Yield: 6 servings

- Soften the gelatin in the cold water in a bowl.
- Add the boiling water, stirring until dissolved.
- Add the sugar and vanilla; mix well.
- Whisk in the sour cream until the mixture is smooth.
- Fold in the whipped topping.
- Pour into a gelatin mold.
- Chill until set.
- Unmold the gelatin onto a serving plate.
- Serve with the Strawberry Topping.
- May substitute sweetened whipped cream for the whipped topping and canned fruit pie filling for the topping.

Strawberry Topping

1 package strawberry Danish dessert mix
1 (10-ounce) package frozen strawberries, or 1 cup sliced fresh strawberries

- Prepare the dessert mix with strawberries using package directions.

Marinated Green Bean Salad

A unique way to replace a lettuce salad.

2 (16-ounce) cans Italian or string
   green beans, drained
1 (8-ounce) jar hearts of palm, drained
1 tomato, chopped
Tarragon Salad Dressing

Yield: 6 servings

- Combine the green beans, hearts of palm and tomato in a bowl; toss lightly to mix.
- Pour the Tarragon Salad Dressing over the salad; toss to mix.
- Marinate, covered, in the refrigerator for at least 4 hours.
- Serve cold.

Tarragon Salad Dressing

1 tablespoon chopped tarragon
1/2 cup red wine vinegar
1/2 cup olive oil
1 tablespoon sugar

- Combine tarragon, vinegar, olive oil and sugar in a bowl; mix well.

Italian Mushroom Salad

Great for a summer picnic.

8 ounces fresh mushrooms, sliced
2 cups sliced zucchini
1 cup cherry tomato halves
1 cup pitted black olives
Spicy Italian Dressing

SPICY ITALIAN DRESSING

1/3 cup olive oil
1/3 cup red wine vinegar
2 tablespoons capers
1 clove of garlic, minced
1/4 teaspoon rosemary, crumbled
1/4 teaspoon oregano, crumbled

Yield: 6 servings

- Combine the mushrooms, zucchini, tomato halves and olives in a bowl; toss gently to mix.
- Pour the Spicy Italian Dressing over the salad; toss to mix.
- Chill, covered, in the refrigerator for 2 to 4 hours before serving.

- Combine the olive oil, vinegar, capers, garlic, rosemary and oregano in a bowl; mix well.

Salad Italiano

*C*ould be served as a light meal.

1 bunch romaine lettuce, chopped

1 small red onion, cut into very thin rings

1 (2-ounce) can sliced black olives, drained

1 (8-ounce) package thinly sliced pepperoni

Italian Salad Dressing

ITALIAN SALAD DRESSING

1 cup mayonnaise

1/3 cup white vinegar

1/2 tablespoon fresh ground pepper

1/2 cup grated Parmesan cheese

1 clove of garlic, minced

Yield: 8 servings

- Combine the romaine lettuce, onion, olives and pepperoni in a large salad bowl; toss lightly to mix.
- Pour the Italian Salad Dressing over the salad just before serving; toss to mix.

- Combine the mayonnaise, vinegar, pepper, Parmesan cheese and garlic in a bowl; mix well.

Summer Tomato Salad

2 tablespoons mayonnaise

2 tablespoons (heaping) sliced green
salad olives with pimentos

2 tablespoons liquid from salad olives

2 tablespoons minced red onion

1 teaspoon sugar

2 large sweet tomatoes

Yield: 2 servings

- Combine the mayonnaise, olives, olive liquid, onion and sugar in a salad bowl; mix well.
- Place the tomatoes on a plate; cut into slices.
- Cut the slices into quarters, reserving the tomato juice.
- Add the tomatoes and juice to the mixture in the salad bowl; toss gently to mix.
- Chill in the refrigerator for 15 minutes or until cool.
- Garnish with a fresh basil leaf.

Catalina Salad

1 1/2 heads leaf lettuce, chopped

1 cup sliced pecans

1 1/2 cups sliced strawberries

Catalina Salad Dressing

Yield: 8 servings

- Combine the lettuce, pecans and strawberries in a large salad bowl; toss to mix.
- Pour the Catalina Salad Dressing over the salad just before serving; toss to mix.

Catalina Salad Dressing

1 cup mayonnaise

1/4 cup white vinegar

1/4 cup honey

2 tablespoons poppy seeds

1 teaspoon vanilla extract

1/2 teaspoon salt

- Combine the mayonnaise, white vinegar, honey, poppy seeds, vanilla and salt in a bowl; mix well.

Hearts of Palm Salad with Herb Dressing

1 (14-ounce) can hearts of palm, drained

1 clove of garlic, peeled

Mixed salad greens

2 cups fresh cherry tomato halves

Herb Dressing

3 tablespoons freshly grated Parmesan cheese

Freshly ground pepper

Yield: 6 servings

- Cut the hearts of palm into 1-inch pieces; drain well.
- Chill until cold.
- Rub a wooden salad bowl with the garlic; discard the garlic.
- Combine the salad greens, cherry tomatoes and hearts of palm in the salad bowl; toss to mix.
- Pour the Herb Dressing over the salad just before serving.
- Add Parmesan cheese and pepper; toss to mix.

Herb Dressing

3/4 cup olive oil

3 tablespoons red wine vinegar

1/4 teaspoon salt

1/4 teaspoon salad herbs

- Combine the olive oil, vinegar, salt and salad herbs in a bowl; mix well.

Popeye's Favorite Salad

Tell the kids the name of the salad and they may be tempted to eat it.

1 package fresh spinach, washed, drained
1/4 head lettuce, torn into bite-size pieces
1 cup bean sprouts
3 hard-cooked eggs, chopped
2 to 3 green onions, chopped
French Salad Dressing
8 slices crisp-cooked bacon, crumbled

Yield: 8 servings

- Combine the spinach, lettuce, bean sprouts, eggs and onions in a bowl; toss to mix.
- Chill, covered, until serving time.
- Pour the French Salad Dressing over the salad; toss to mix.
- Sprinkle the crumbled bacon over the top.

French Salad Dressing

1 cup vegetable oil
3/4 cup sugar
1/3 cup catsup
1/4 cup vinegar
1 teaspoon Worcestershire sauce
1/4 teaspoon salt

- Whisk together the oil, sugar, catsup, vinegar, Worcestershire sauce and salt in a bowl.
- Chill, covered, until serving time.

Mom's Coleslaw

1 head cabbage
2 carrots, grated
1 onion, grated
1/4 cup vinegar
2 tablespoons sugar
3/4 cup mayonnaise-type salad dressing
Paprika

Yield: 10 servings

- Process the cabbage in a food processor until finely chopped. Combine with the carrots and onion in a bowl; mix well.
- Mix the vinegar and sugar in a bowl. Pour over the cabbage mixture. Let stand for 5 minutes.
- Add the salad dressing; mix well. Spoon into a serving dish. Sprinkle with paprika. Chill, covered, until serving time.

Grape and Havarti Salad

A nice summer salad.

1 bunch Bibb lettuce, chopped
1 bunch leaf lettuce, chopped
10 to 15 each green and red grapes
Sections of 1 orange
1/2 to 3/4 cup cubed Havarti cheese
Sweet-and-Sour Dressing

Yield: 12 servings

- Combine the Bibb lettuce, leaf lettuce, green grapes, red grapes, orange sections and cheese in a salad bowl; mix well.
- Chill, covered, until serving time. Toss the Sweet-and-Sour Dressing with the salad just before serving.

SWEET-AND-SOUR DRESSING

1 (6-ounce) can frozen orange juice concentrate
1/4 cup honey
1/2 cup vegetable oil
1/4 teaspoon ginger

- Process the orange juice concentrate, honey, oil and ginger in a blender until well blended.

Curried Fruit and Nut Salad

Curry lovers will want an extra helping.

1 bunch red leaf lettuce or romaine
  lettuce, chopped
1 cup torn fresh spinach
1 (11-ounce) can mandarin oranges,
  drained
1 cup seedless grapes
½ cup toasted slivered almonds
Curried Dressing
1 avocado, peeled, sliced

Yield: 12 servings

- Combine the leaf lettuce, spinach, mandarin oranges, grapes and almonds in a large salad bowl; toss to mix.
- Chill, covered, until serving time.
- Toss the Curried Dressing with the salad just before serving.
- Top with the avocado.

Curried Dressing

½ cup vegetable oil
⅓ cup white wine vinegar
1 clove of garlic, minced
2 tablespoons brown sugar
2 tablespoons minced chives
1 tablespoon curry powder
1 teaspoon soy sauce

- Mix the oil, vinegar, garlic, brown sugar, chives, curry powder and soy sauce in a bowl.

Mandarin Salad

1 head lettuce or 1 pound fresh
    spinach, chopped

1 cup chopped celery

1/2 cup green onions, chopped

1 (11-ounce) can mandarin oranges,
    drained

8 ounces mozzarella cheese, shredded

1/2 cup sliced almonds

2 tablespoons sugar

Poppy Seed Dressing

POPPY SEED DRESSING

1/3 cup sugar

5 tablespoons white vinegar

1 teaspoon salt

1 1/2 teaspoons minced onion

1 1/2 teaspoons poppy seeds

1 cup vegetable oil

Yield: 12 servings

- Combine the lettuce, celery, green onions, mandarin oranges and cheese in a salad bowl.
- Sauté the almonds with 2 tablespoons sugar in a nonstick skillet until brown, stirring constantly.
- Add to the salad; toss to mix.
- Chill, covered, until serving time.
- Toss the Poppy Seed Dressing with the salad just before serving.

- Combine 1/3 cup sugar, vinegar, salt, minced onion and poppy seeds in a small bowl; mix well.
- Add the oil; mix well.

Avocado Grapefruit Salad

Dressing may be kept in the refrigerator for two weeks.

Mixed salad greens, including romaine
  and Bibb lettuce, chopped
1 avocado, peeled, sliced
Sections of 1 grapefruit
1 red onion, sliced into rings
Toasted slivered almonds
Spicy Dressing

SPICY DRESSING

¼ cup vegetable oil
2 tablespoons red wine vinegar
1 teaspoon Worcestershire sauce
½ teaspoon salt
Parsley flakes
Freshly ground pepper to taste

Yield: 6 servings

- Combine the salad greens, avocado, grapefruit, onion and almonds in a salad bowl; toss to mix.
- Chill, covered, until serving time.
- Toss the Spicy Dressing with the salad just before serving.

- Combine the oil, vinegar, Worcestershire sauce, salt, parsley flakes and pepper in a bowl; mix well.

Curried Spinach Salad

2 pounds fresh spinach
3 unpeeled Red or Golden Delicious
  apples
³/₄ cup dry-roasted Spanish peanuts
¹/₂ cup dried cherries
2 tablespoons sesame seeds
Curried Chutney Dressing

Yield: 20 servings

- Rinse the spinach; discard the tough leaves and stems.
- Pat dry with paper towels.
- Tear into bite-size pieces into a container.
- Chill, covered, until cold.
- Remove the cores from the apples just before serving.
- Cut the apples into slices.
- Combine the spinach, apple slices, peanuts, cherries and sesame seeds in a salad bowl; toss to mix.
- Pour the Curried Chutney Dressing over the salad; toss to mix.

CURRIED CHUTNEY DRESSING

2 tablespoons white wine vinegar
²/₃ cup vegetable oil
1 tablespoon finely chopped chutney
1 teaspoon curry powder
1 teaspoon salt
1 teaspoon dry mustard
¹/₄ teaspoon hot pepper sauce

- Combine the vinegar, oil, chutney, curry powder, salt, dry mustard and hot pepper sauce in a bowl; mix well.
- Let stand, covered, at room temperature for at least 2 hours.

Strawberry Spinach Salad

1 (1-pound) package fresh spinach
1 pint fresh strawberries
Small rings of ½ sliced red onion
Raspberry Vinaigrette

Yield: 12 servings

- Rinse the spinach; discard the stems.
- Pat the spinach dry with paper towels; tear into bite-size pieces.
- Chill, covered, until serving time.
- Cut the strawberries into slices, reserving several whole strawberries for the top.
- Combine the spinach, strawberries and small onion rings in a large salad bowl just before serving; toss to mix.
- Pour the Raspberry Vinaigrette over the salad; toss to mix.
- Cut the reserved strawberries into fan shapes and arrange over the top.

Raspberry Vinaigrette

½ cup sugar
2 teaspoons salt
2 teaspoons dry mustard
⅔ cup raspberry vinegar
3 tablespoons chopped red onion
2 cups safflower oil
¾ tablespoon poppy seeds

- Combine the sugar, salt, dry mustard, raspberry vinegar, chopped onion, oil and poppy seeds in a bowl; mix well.

Avocado Raspberry Salad

2½ cups shredded napa cabbage
1½ cups shredded red cabbage
2 tomatoes, cut into wedges
1 avocado, cubed
½ cucumber, thinly sliced
2 tablespoons chopped green onions
Raspberry Jam Dressing

RASPBERRY JAM DRESSING

¼ cup seedless red raspberry jam
3 tablespoons vegetable oil
2½ tablespoons white wine vinegar
¾ teaspoon lemon pepper seasoning
¾ teaspoon seasoned salt

Yield: 4 servings

- Mound the napa and red cabbage on 4 individual salad plates.
- Arrange the tomatoes, avocado and cucumber over the cabbage.
- Sprinkle the green onions over the top.
- Drizzle the Raspberry Jam Dressing on each salad.

- Combine the raspberry jam, oil, vinegar, lemon pepper seasoning and seasoned salt in a bowl; mix well.

Hot Dutch Potato Salad*

1 pound leaf lettuce, shredded
1 small onion, chopped
Salt and pepper to taste
6 slices bacon, finely chopped
1/4 cup vinegar
2 tablespoons sugar
1/2 cup water
2 tablespoons flour
1 tablespoon mustard
1 egg
4 hot cooked medium potatoes, mashed
2 hard-cooked eggs, sliced

Yield: 10 servings

- Combine the lettuce, onion, salt and pepper in a large salad bowl.
- Fry the bacon in a skillet until fat is rendered.
- Remove the bacon and drain, reserving 3 tablespoons bacon drippings in skillet.
- Blend the vinegar, sugar, water, flour, mustard and 1 egg in a bowl.
- Add to the reserved bacon drippings.
- Cook over medium heat until the mixture is thickened, stirring constantly.
- Add the hot mashed potatoes to the lettuce mixture.
- Pour the hot dressing over the salad; add the hard-cooked eggs.
- Toss to mix.
- Top with reserved bacon.

Garden Potato Salad

Nice change-of-pace potato salad.

½ cup white wine vinegar

½ cup light olive oil

1 teaspoon Dijon mustard

1 clove of garlic, minced

½ teaspoon salt

¼ teaspoon freshly ground pepper

1 teaspoon sugar

3 pounds unpeeled new red potatoes

Flowerets of ½ head cauliflower

Florets of ½ head broccoli

8 ounces snow peas, cut into halves diagonally

1 medium red bell pepper, cut into rings

⅔ cup chopped celery

⅓ cup chopped fresh parsley

Yield: 15 servings

- Combine the vinegar, olive oil, mustard, garlic, salt, pepper and sugar in a large bowl; mix well.
- Cook the red potatoes in water to cover in a saucepan over medium heat just until tender; drain.
- Rinse in cold water. Cut into fourths.
- Add to the dressing; toss to coat.
- Steam the cauliflower, broccoli and snow peas just until tender-crisp; drain.
- Rinse in cold water. Add to the potatoes.
- Add the red pepper, celery and parsley; toss to mix.
- Chill, covered, in the refrigerator.
- Let stand at room temperature for 30 minutes before serving.

Sla Stamppot*

A popular Dutch lettuce dish of the 1890s.

1 pound potatoes, peeled
Salt to taste
1 pound leaf lettuce, chopped
1 cup radish slices
1 cup chopped celery
1/2 cup chopped cucumber
1 small onion, finely chopped
2 tablespoons melted butter
1/4 cup vinegar
8 ounces bacon, chopped
3 eggs

Yield: 10 servings

- Cook the potatoes in enough salted water to cover in a saucepan over medium heat until tender; drain, reserving 1/4 cup water.
- Mash potatoes just enough to break into fine pieces.
- Combine the lettuce, radish slices, celery, cucumber and onion in a large salad bowl.
- Combine the butter, vinegar and reserved potato water in a small saucepan.
- Fry the bacon in a skillet until crisp.
- Reserve enough bacon drippings in the skillet to fry the eggs; add the remaining bacon drippings and bacon to the butter in the saucepan.
- Fry the eggs in the reserved bacon drippings in the skillet until cooked through; cut into fine strips.
- Add the hot eggs, hot potatoes and butter mixture to the lettuce in the salad bowl; mix well.
- Serve immediately.

Tabouli

1 cup dry bulgur

1½ cups boiling water

1½ teaspoons salt

¼ cup fresh lemon juice

1 teaspoon (heaping) fresh crushed garlic

½ cup chopped scallions with tops

½ teaspoon dried mint

¼ cup olive oil

2 medium tomatoes, chopped

1 cup packed chopped fresh parsley

½ cup cooked chick-peas (optional)

½ cup grated carrot (optional)

½ cup chopped green bell pepper (optional)

1 cup chopped cucumber (optional)

Yield: 4 servings

- Combine the bulgur, boiling water and salt in a bowl.
- Let stand, covered, for 15 to 20 minutes.
- Add the lemon juice, garlic, scallions, mint and olive oil; mix well.
- Chill, covered, for 2 to 3 hours.
- Add the tomatoes, parsley and any of the optional ingredients desired; toss to mix.

Artichoke Rice Medley Salad

1 (8-ounce) package chicken-flavor
Rice-A-Roni

2¼ cups water

2 (6-ounce) jars marinated artichoke
hearts

¼ cup chopped pimento-stuffed olives
(optional)

2 large green onions, sliced

1 (8-ounce) can water chestnuts,
drained

⅓ cup mayonnaise

¼ teaspoon curry powder

¼ teaspoon salt

Freshly ground pepper

Yield: 10 servings

- Cook the rice with 2¼ cups water using package directions. Place in a large bowl.
- Drain the artichoke hearts, reserving the marinade.
- Chop the artichokes coarsely. Add the artichokes, olives and green onions to the rice.
- Rinse the water chestnuts; drain. Chop into fine pieces. Add to the rice.
- Combine the reserved marinade, mayonnaise, curry powder, salt and pepper in a small bowl; mix well.
- Stir into the warm rice.
- Serve warm or chilled.
- The salad will keep in the refrigerator for up to 2 days.
- May mold the salad in a 5- to 6-cup ring mold.

Celery Seed Dressing

A wonderful way to top mixed fresh fruit.

⅓ cup sugar

1 teaspoon salt

1 teaspoon dry mustard

1 teaspoon grated onion

¼ cup vinegar

1 cup vegetable oil

1 teaspoon celery seeds

Yield: 1½ cups

- Combine the sugar, salt and dry mustard in a bowl; mix well.
- Stir in the onion and vinegar. Add the oil 1 tablespoon at a time, beating constantly.
- Stir in the celery seeds.

POPPY SEED SWEET-AND-SOUR DRESSING

1 cup sugar

1 teaspoon salt

3 tablespoons onion juice or 2 dashes onion powder

2 teaspoons dry mustard

2/3 cup vinegar

3 cups vegetable oil

3 tablespoons poppy seeds

Yield: 4¹/2 cups

- Combine the sugar, salt, onion juice, mustard and vinegar in a bowl; mix well.
- Add the oil gradually, beating constantly.
- Stir in the poppy seeds.
- Serve over mushrooms, strawberries, sugared sliced almonds, pineapple or greens.

POPPY SEED DRESSING

Serve over a spinach salad.

3/4 cup honey

1 teaspoon salt

3/4 cup vinegar

6 tablespoons mustard

6 tablespoons poppy seeds

2¹/2 cups vegetable oil

1 medium onion, finely chopped

Yield: 4 cups

- Combine the honey, salt, vinegar, mustard and poppy seeds in a bowl; mix well.
- Add the oil gradually, beating constantly. Stir in the onion.
- Store, covered, in the refrigerator.

Swedish Tomato Mayonnaise

Will keep for several weeks in the refrigerator. Stir before using.

1/2 cup garlic, roasted in olive oil
1 cup mayonnaise
1/4 cup rehydrated sun-dried tomatoes
Freshly ground pepper, optional
Fresh lemon juice, optional

Yield: 1³/₄ cups

- Process the garlic, mayonnaise, sun-dried tomatoes, pepper and lemon juice in a blender until puréed.
- Store, covered, in the refrigerator.

Herbed Mustard

Drizzle over fish, beef or pork. Serve with mushrooms or tiny eggplant.

1 cup dry mustard
1 cup white wine tarragon vinegar or
    other herbed vinegar
3/4 cup sugar
3 egg yolks
Lemon juice to taste

Yield: 3 cups

- Combine the dry mustard and vinegar in a bowl; mix well.
- Let stand, covered, for 2 hours to overnight.
- Spoon into a double boiler.
- Stir in the sugar and egg yolks.
- Cook over hot water until thickened, stirring constantly.
- Stir in lemon juice.
- Chill, covered, before serving.

Champagne Mustard

You'll find yourself using this on everything you serve.

²/₃ cup Champagne vinegar
¹/₂ cup dry mustard
1 cup sugar
3 eggs

Yield: 2¹/₂ cups

- Combine the vinegar, dry mustard, sugar and eggs in a double boiler; beat well.
- Cook over hot water just until thickened, stirring constantly.
- Do not overcook; mustard will become rubbery.

Honey French Dressing

Serve over a green salad or fruit.

¹/₃ cup honey
¹/₃ cup vegetable oil
¹/₃ cup vinegar
¹/₃ teaspoon catsup
¹/₂ teaspoon salt
¹/₂ teaspoon pepper
¹/₂ teaspoon celery seeds
¹/₂ teaspoon paprika

Yield: 1 cup

- Combine the honey, oil, vinegar, catsup, salt, pepper, celery seeds and paprika in a blender container.
- Process until blended.
- Store, covered, in the refrigerator.
- Shake well before using.

BALSAMIC AND DIJON DRESSING

1 large shallot, minced
1 teaspoon Dijon mustard
2 tablespoons balsamic vinegar
1 tablespoon lemon juice
6 tablespoons virgin olive oil
Salt and pepper to taste

Yield: 3/4 cup

- Combine the shallot, mustard, vinegar and lemon juice in a bowl; mix well.
- Add the olive oil gradually, whisking constantly.
- Add salt and pepper.

HERBY GARLIC CROUTONS

3 tablespoons unsalted butter
3 tablespoons olive oil
3 cups cubed dried bread
2 cloves of garlic, minced
1 teaspoon chopped fresh parsley
1 teaspoon chopped chives
1 teaspoon tarragon
3 tablespoons grated Parmesan cheese

Yield: 3 cups

- Heat the butter and olive oil in a skillet over medium heat until the butter is melted.
- Add the bread cubes. Sauté for 3 to 4 minutes, tossing to coat.
- Add the garlic, parsley, chives and tarragon.
- Cook until golden brown, stirring constantly.
- Combine the mixture with the Parmesan cheese in a bowl, tossing until the bread is coated.
- Cool to room temperature.
- Store, covered, in an airtight container.

THE DINNER HOUR

HOLLAND'S UNIQUE DOWNTOWN AT NIGHT; INCLUDES
HISTORIC TOWER CLOCK, RESTORED AND RENOVATED SHOPS, FEATURES
"SNOWMELT" SNOW-FREE SIDEWALKS AND STREETS.

A crisp Autumn evening in Downtown Holland.

The Dinner Hour

*Most requested recipe
from **Eet Smakelijk**

RED CABBAGE*
(Rode Kool)

2 pounds red cabbage, shredded
5 to 6 sour apples, peeled, sliced
1½ cups water
½ cup packed light brown sugar
½ cup pickled peach juice
¼ cup butter
1½ teaspoons salt

Yield: 6 servings

- Combine the cabbage, apples and water in a large saucepan.
- Cook, covered, just until the apples are tender, stirring occasionally.
- Add the brown sugar, peach juice, butter and salt.
- Cook, uncovered, for 5 minutes longer.

PINEAPPLE-GLAZED CARROTS

6 large carrots, sliced
1 (8-ounce) can crushed pineapple, drained
¼ cup butter
½ cup orange juice
½ cup packed light brown sugar

Yield: 6 to 8 servings

- Combine the carrots, pineapple, butter, orange juice and brown sugar in a baking dish.
- Bake, tightly covered, at 350 degrees for 1 hour.

Vanilla Carrot Mousse

2½ cups carrots, peeled, cut into
½-inch pieces

3 tablespoons butter or margarine

3 tablespoons flour

1½ cups apple juice

2 to 3 teaspoons vanilla extract

¾ teaspoon salt

⅛ teaspoon pepper

¼ teaspoon nutmeg

Yield: 5 to 6 servings

- Combine the carrots with enough water to cover in a medium saucepan. Bring to a boil.
- Cook, covered, for 12 to 14 minutes or until the carrots are tender; drain.
- Mash the carrots with a potato masher in a medium bowl; set aside.
- Melt the butter in a medium saucepan. Stir in the flour. Cook for 1 minute, stirring constantly.
- Stir in the apple juice, vanilla, salt, pepper and nutmeg.
- Bring to a boil; remove from heat.
- Add the carrots and mix well.
- Spoon the mixture into a 2-quart baking dish that has been greased or sprayed with nonstick cooking spray.
- Bake at 350 degrees for 15 minutes or until bubbly and heated through.

Easy Cheesy Cauliflower

This is a quick microwave side dish.

1 head cauliflower, cut into flowerets
1/2 cup mayonnaise-type salad dressing
1 teaspoon chopped onion
1 teaspoon mustard
1/2 cup shredded Cheddar cheese

Yield: 2 to 3 servings

- Place the cauliflower on a microwave-safe plate and cover with plastic wrap. Microwave on High for 9 minutes.
- Let the cauliflower stand for 5 minutes.
- Mix the salad dressing, onion and mustard in a bowl.
- Pour the mixture over the cauliflower.
- Sprinkle with the cheese.
- Microwave on Medium for 2 minutes.

Baked Chile Cheese Corn

This is a fun accompaniment for tacos.

4 cups corn
1 cup shredded Cheddar cheese
8 ounces cream cheese, softened
1 (4-ounce) can chopped green chiles
2 teaspoons chili powder
2 teaspoons cumin

Yield: 4 to 6 servings

- Mix the corn, Cheddar cheese, cream cheese, green chiles, chili powder and cumin in a bowl.
- Spoon the mixture into a greased 1 1/2-quart baking dish.
- Bake at 350 degrees for 20 minutes.

Alpen Rose Idaho Potato Torta

The Alpen Rose, nestled in the heart of downtown Holland, serves a wide array of Austrian cuisine.

1 tablespoon olive oil

½ cup minced onion

6 tomatoes, peeled, sliced

⅔ cup basil leaves, shredded

½ cup olive oil

Salt and pepper to taste

1 eggplant, cut into ¼-inch slices

1 zucchini, cut into ¼-inch slices

2 large yellow onions, cut into ¼-inch slices

3 red bell peppers, cut into halves

6 whole cloves of garlic

3 tablespoons olive oil

1 cup sliced mushrooms

6 Idaho potatoes, cut into quarters

1 cup skim milk, heated

1½ cups bread crumbs

6 tablespoons grated nonfat Parmesan cheese

1½ pints mixed salad greens

½ cup cooked black beans

2 tablespoons red wine vinegar

¼ cup olive oil

Yield: 6 servings

- Heat the 1 tablespoon olive oil in a saucepan.
- Add the minced onion.
- Cook until the onion is translucent but not browned.
- Add the sliced tomatoes.
- Simmer over low heat for 35 to 40 minutes or until slightly thickened.
- Purée in a food processor; return the purée to the saucepan.
- Add half the basil; keep warm.
- Mix the ½ cup oil with salt and pepper.
- Brush over the eggplant, zucchini, sliced onions and red peppers.
- Grill the eggplant and zucchini over hot coals until scored by the grill but not cooked through; keep warm.
- Place the red peppers, sliced onions and garlic on a baking sheet.
- Roast at 400 degrees for 20 to 30 minutes or until tender and evenly browned.
- Keep the onions and garlic warm.
- Place the red peppers in a plastic bag to cool. Peel and cut into wide strips.
- Heat the 3 tablespoons olive oil in a skillet. Add the mushrooms. Sauté for 5 minutes. Season with salt and pepper and remove from heat.

(Continued on next page)

Alpen Rose Idaho Potato Torta *(Continued)*

- Mix the mushrooms with the roasted onions; let stand to cool.
- Combine the potatoes with enough water to cover in a saucepan.
- Boil until the potatoes are tender; drain.
- Purée the potatoes with the roasted garlic in a food processor.
- Add the hot milk, salt and pepper.
- Combine the remaining basil, bread crumbs and cheese in a bowl.
- Press half the cheese mixture into a nonstick 9-inch springform pan.
- Top with the grilled eggplant and zucchini.
- Layer ⅓ of the potatoes, the roasted peppers, ⅓ of the potatoes, the mushroom mixture and the remaining potatoes over the zucchini.
- Press the remaining cheese mixture over the top.
- Cover the torta loosely with parchment.
- Bake at 350 degrees for 30 to 35 minutes or until heated through; remove the parchment.
- Bake for 6 to 8 minutes longer or until the cheese mixture forms a crisp golden crust.
- Remove from the oven and let stand for 15 minutes.
- Toss the salad greens with the black beans in a bowl.
- Add the vinegar and ¼ cup olive oil and adjust the seasonings. Toss until evenly coated.
- Unmold the torta; slice into 6 wedges.
- Spoon some of the tomato sauce on each plate; top with a wedge of torta.
- Arrange the salad on the side.

Aardappel Pof*
(Potato Puff)

2 cups mashed potatoes
3 tablespoons light cream
2 tablespoons butter
2 egg yolks
1/2 teaspoon salt
1/8 teaspoon pepper, or to taste
2 egg whites, stiffly beaten

Yield: 4 to 6 servings
- Combine the potatoes, cream, butter, egg yolks, salt and pepper in a skillet.
- Cook until heated through, stirring until well blended.
- Fold in the egg whites. Spoon the mixture into a greased 1½-quart baking dish.
- Bake at 375 degrees until golden brown.

Spinach Souffle

This easy vegetable dish looks impressive on your table.

8 ounces cream cheese
1/4 cup butter
2 (10-ounce) packages frozen chopped spinach, thawed, drained
1 cup herb-seasoned stuffing mix

Yield: 6 servings
- Melt the cream cheese and butter in a double boiler over hot water.
- Mix with the spinach and spoon into a greased shallow baking pan.
- Sprinkle with the stuffing mix and dot with additional butter.
- Bake at 350 degrees for 30 minutes.

Sweet Potato Crunch

3 cups mashed cooked sweet potatoes
1 teaspoon vanilla extract
$1/3$ cup melted margarine
1 cup packed brown sugar
1 cup flaked coconut
1 cup chopped pecans
$1/3$ cup melted margarine
$1/3$ cup flour

Yield: 4 to 6 servings

- Combine the sweet potatoes, vanilla and $1/3$ cup margarine in a bowl.
- Spoon the mixture into a greased $1^{1}/2$-quart casserole.
- Mix the brown sugar, coconut, pecans, $1/3$ cup margarine and flour in a bowl.
- Sprinkle over the sweet potato mixture.
- Bake, covered, at 350 degrees for 20 minutes.
- Bake, uncovered, for 15 minutes longer.

Green Beans with Tomatoes

2 pounds fresh green beans, trimmed
1 can pasta-style chunky tomatoes
1 can stewed tomatoes
$1/3$ cup olive oil
1 teaspoon basil
1 to 2 tablespoons fresh garlic
Salt and pepper to taste

Yield: 6 servings

- Steam the beans in a small amount of water in a large saucepan until tender; drain and return the beans to the pan.
- Add the tomatoes, olive oil, basil, garlic, salt and pepper; mix well.
- Cook until heated through.

Zucchini and Artichoke Heart Casserole

1 to 2 cloves of garlic, minced
1 small onion, minced
1/2 green bell pepper, chopped
3 to 4 tablespoons salad oil
1 (8-ounce) can artichoke hearts, drained, rinsed, cut into quarters
1 to 2 small zucchini, sliced horizontally
1/2 teaspoon salt, or to taste
1/4 teaspoon pepper, or to taste
1/4 to 1/2 cup freshly grated Parmesan cheese

Yield: 4 to 6 servings

- Brown the garlic, onion and green pepper in the oil in a skillet.
- Remove the vegetables from the skillet and keep warm.
- Sauté the artichoke hearts and zucchini in the pan drippings in the skillet.
- Season with the salt and pepper.
- Stir in the garlic mixture; spoon into a baking dish.
- Sprinkle with the cheese.
- Bake at 350 degrees for 5 to 10 minutes or until the cheese is melted and coats the vegetables.

Zucchini and Squash Provençale

2 (16-ounce) cans stewed tomatoes
2 cups sliced zucchini
1 onion, sliced
$^1/_2$ cup quick-cooking white rice
1 tablespoon margarine, chopped
2 cups chopped small yellow squash
$^3/_4$ teaspoon garlic salt
$^1/_2$ teaspoon pepper
2 tablespoons margarine, chopped
8 ounces mozzarella cheese, shredded
2 tablespoons grated Parmesan cheese

Yield: 6 to 8 servings

- Drain the tomatoes, reserving $^1/_4$ cup of the juice.
- Arrange the zucchini in a 9x13-inch baking dish and top with the onion slices.
- Sprinkle the rice over the onion.
- Dot with the 1 tablespoon margarine and top with the squash.
- Add the tomatoes, garlic salt, pepper and reserved tomato juice.
- Dot with 2 tablespoons margarine.
- Bake, tightly covered with foil, at 350 degrees for 50 minutes.
- Remove the foil and top the casserole with the mozzarella cheese and Parmesan cheese.
- Bake, uncovered, for 5 to 10 minutes or until the cheese is melted.

Brown Rice Pilaf

2 tablespoons butter
¼ cup vegetable oil
1 medium onion, minced
2 large stalks celery, coarsely chopped
4 cups cooked brown rice
¾ cup dried tart cherries
½ cup coarsely chopped pecans
¾ cup finely chopped scallions
Salt and pepper to taste

Yield: 8 servings

- Melt the butter with the vegetable oil in a large skillet; add the onion to the skillet.
- Cook until the onion is soft and translucent.
- Add the celery. Cook for several minutes.
- Stir in the rice.
- Cook for several minutes longer, stirring constantly; remove from heat.
- Stir in the cherries, pecans and scallions quickly.
- Season with the salt and pepper.

Tom Nienhuis's Risi Bisi

We are lucky to have one of the country's finest chefs, Tom Nienhuis, right here in Holland.

¹/₄ cup vegetable oil

1 medium onion, chopped

1 cup rice

2 cups chicken stock

1 green bell pepper, chopped

1 red bell pepper, chopped

4 ounces mushrooms, chopped

¹/₂ cup cooked green peas

Yield: 3 to 4 servings

- Heat the oil in a deep skillet or stockpot.
- Add the onion and rice.
- Sauté for 5 minutes.
- Add the chicken stock.
- Bring the mixture to a boil
- Spoon mixture into 2-quart casserole dish.
- Bake, covered, at 350 degrees for 20 minutes.
- Sauté the bell peppers, mushrooms and green peas in a skillet.
- Stir into the baked mixture.

Skiers' Beef Brisket

A great way to feed a group of hungry skiers.

1 (4-pound) beef brisket
Olive oil
1¹/₂ teaspoons salt
1¹/₂ teaspoons pepper
2 tablespoons chili powder
1 teaspoon crushed bay leaf
3 tablespoons brown sugar
1 (14-ounce) bottle catsup
¹/₂ cup water
1 tablespoon hot dry mustard
2 teaspoons celery seeds
6 tablespoons butter
¹/₄ teaspoon cayenne
Salt and pepper to taste

Yield: 12 to 15 servings

- Rub the brisket with the olive oil.
- Place the brisket fat side up in a large roasting pan.
- Mix the 1¹/₂ teaspoons salt, 1¹/₂ teaspoons pepper, chili powder and bay leaf in a bowl.
- Rub the mixture over the top of the brisket.
- Bake, tightly covered, at 325 degrees for 4¹/₂ hours.
- Scrape off the seasoning; cut the brisket cross grain into very thin slices.
- Combine the brown sugar, catsup, water, dry mustard, celery seeds, butter, cayenne and salt and pepper to taste in a saucepan.
- Bring to a boil, stirring occasionally.
- Cook for 10 minutes.
- Serve the sauce with the sliced brisket.

Charcoal Roast

Great on the grill.

Unseasoned tenderizer
1 (2⅓-pound) chuck roast
½ cup plus 2 tablespoons soy sauce
¼ cup packed brown sugar
1 tablespoon Worcestershire sauce
1 tablespoon lemon juice
1½ cups water

Yield: 6 to 10 servings

- Tenderize the roast using the package directions.
- Combine the soy sauce, brown sugar, Worcestershire sauce, lemon juice and water in a jar; cover and shake well.
- Pour over the roast in a large bowl.
- Marinate, covered, for 8 to 12 hours.
- Grill for 10 minutes per side.

Mustard-Glazed Corned Beef

1 (6-pound) corned beef
1 medium onion, cut into halves
1 stalk celery, chopped
2 cloves of garlic, cut into halves
½ teaspoon peppercorns
⅔ cup packed brown sugar
2 tablespoons prepared mustard
2 tablespoons catsup

Yield: 12 to 15 servings

- Combine the beef, onion, celery, garlic and peppercorns with enough water to cover in an 8-quart saucepan.
- Bring to a boil over high heat; reduce the heat to low. Simmer, covered, for 3 hours or until the beef is tender.
- Cut the beef into slices; arrange overlapping slices on an ovenproof platter or in an open roasting pan.
- Mix the brown sugar, mustard and catsup in a bowl.
- Spread the mixture over and between the slices of beef.
- Bake at 350 degrees for 20 minutes or until the glaze is browned.

Flank Steak with Dressing

The rolled steak looks elegant, and the flavor is terrific.

1 flank steak
1 teaspoon salt
1/8 teaspoon paprika
1/8 teaspoon ginger
1/4 teaspoon mustard
1 teaspoon Worcestershire sauce
1/4 cup butter or margarine
2 tablespoons chopped onion
1 cup bread crumbs
1/4 teaspoon salt
1/8 teaspoon paprika
2 tablespoons chopped parsley
3 tablespoons chopped celery
1 egg, slightly beaten
3 tablespoons margarine
2 tablespoons flour
1 cup water or beef stock
1 cup tomato juice or dry white wine
1/4 teaspoon salt

Yield: 4 servings

- Trim the edges of the steak.
- Season the steak with a mixture of the 1 teaspoon salt, 1/8 teaspoon paprika, ginger, mustard and Worcestershire sauce.
- Melt the 1/4 cup butter in a skillet. Add the onion. Sauté until the onion is browned.
- Add the bread crumbs, 1/4 teaspoon salt, 1/8 teaspoon paprika, parsley, celery and egg; mix well.
- Spread the dressing over the steak; roll the steak loosely and tie it.
- Heat the 3 tablespoons margarine in a skillet.
- Add the steak.
- Cook until the steak is seared on all sides.
- Remove the steak to a casserole or loosely covered dish, reserving the pan drippings.
- Stir the flour into the pan drippings in the skillet.
- Add the water, tomato juice and 1/4 teaspoon salt.
- Pour the mixture over the steak.
- Bake at 250 degrees for 1 1/2 hours, adjusting the seasonings as needed.
- Serve with a green vegetable.

Orange Sauce and Beef Stir-Fry

1 (12-ounce) top round steak
1 tablespoon cornstarch
1 teaspoon sugar
1 teaspoon instant beef bouillon
1 teaspoon finely shredded orange peel
1/2 cup orange juice
1 tablespoon soy sauce
4 green onions
1 clove of garlic, minced
1 tablespoon olive oil
6 cups torn fresh spinach
1/3 cup sliced water chestnuts
2 cups hot cooked rice

Yield: 2 to 3 servings

- Slice the steak cross grain into thin bite-size strips.
- Combine the cornstarch, sugar and beef bouillon in a small bowl.
- Stir in the orange peel, orange juice and soy sauce.
- Spray a wok with nonstick cooking spray and heat over medium heat.
- Stir-fry the green onions and garlic in the wok for 1 minute; remove the vegetables and set aside.
- Pour the olive oil into the wok and add the beef strips.
- Stir-fry for 2 to 3 minutes or until the beef is cooked through; remove the beef from the wok.
- Stir the orange sauce into the center of the wok.
- Cook until the sauce is thickened and bubbly, stirring constantly.
- Stir in the spinach, water chestnuts, green onion mixture and beef.
- Cook, covered, for 1 minute or until heated through.
- Serve over the rice.

French Onion and Beef Strudel

This is almost too beautiful to cut into.

1/4 cup margarine

1 1/2 cups sliced onions

6 ounces beef tenderloin or sirloin, cut into 1/8-inch slices

1 teaspoon flour

1 teaspoon brown sugar

1/2 teaspoon cumin

1/4 teaspoon salt

1/4 teaspoon pepper

1/2 cup beef broth

1 (8-count) can crescent rolls

1/4 cup freshly grated Parmesan cheese

3/4 cup shredded mozzarella cheese

2 tablespoons freshly grated Parmesan cheese

1/2 cup plain yogurt

1 (10-ounce) can au jus gravy, heated

Yield: 4 servings

- Melt the margarine in a heavy skillet over medium heat. Add the onions. Cook for 15 to 20 minutes or until the onions are brown, stirring constantly. Remove the onions with a slotted spoon to a medium bowl.

- Add the beef to the skillet. Cook for 2 to 3 minutes or until the beef is evenly browned, stirring constantly. Return the onions and any juice to the skillet.

- Add the flour, brown sugar, cumin, salt, pepper and broth; mix well. Cook for 5 minutes or until most of the liquid is absorbed, scraping the skillet frequently.

- Separate the dough into 8 triangles. Overlap the long sides of 2 triangles slightly to make 1 large triangle, pressing the edges to seal. Repeat the procedure with the remaining triangles. Place the triangles, slightly overlapping, in a row on a greased baking sheet.

- Spoon the onion mixture evenly down the center of the triangles in a 1 1/2-inch wide strip, beginning and ending 1 inch from the ends.

- Sprinkle a mixture of 1/4 cup Parmesan cheese and the mozzarella cheese over the onion mixture. Bring the side points over the filling, crossing one over the other to produce a braided appearance; seal the ends.

- Sprinkle with 2 tablespoons Parmesan cheese.

- Bake at 375 degrees for 15 to 20 minutes or until deep golden brown.

- Serve hot with dollops of yogurt and gravy for dipping.

Snowy Day Lamb Stew

This is guaranteed to warm you up.

2½ pounds lamb, boned, trimmed
¼ cup olive oil
1 onion, coarsely chopped
1 clove of garlic, minced
2 tablespoons flour
1½ cups chicken broth
1½ teaspoons salt
⅛ teaspoon pepper, or to taste
¼ teaspoon marjoram
1 bay leaf, crumbled
2 tablespoons lemon juice
4 carrots, chopped
4 potatoes, peeled, cut into quarters
1 (16-ounce) can small white onions

Yield: 4 to 6 servings

- Brown the lamb in the olive oil in a skillet; remove the lamb and set aside.
- Drain the skillet, leaving a small amount of the oil in the skillet.
- Sauté the chopped onion and garlic in the oil in the skillet.
- Add the lamb, flour, broth, salt, pepper, marjoram, bay leaf and lemon juice; mix well.
- Simmer, covered, for 5 minutes.
- Add the carrots, potatoes and canned onions; mix well.
- Simmer for 25 minutes.
- Garnish with parsley.

Blinde Vinken*

A hearty, Dutch favorite.

1 whole pork tenderloin
12 ounces unseasoned pork sausage
12 ounces ground chuck
1/4 teaspoon salt
1/4 teaspoon pepper
1 teaspoon Kitchen Bouquet
2 eggs, slightly beaten
1/4 cup rusk crumbs
1/4 cup light cream
8 slices bacon
1/4 cup margarine
2 tablespoons water
8 ounces fresh mushrooms, sliced
1/4 cup chopped onion
2 tablespoons margarine

Yield: 6 to 8 servings

- Split the tenderloin horizontally almost all the way through.
- Pound the pork gently to a thickness of 1/4 inch and cut into 3x5-inch pieces.
- Combine the sausage, ground chuck, salt, pepper, Kitchen Bouquet, eggs, crumbs and cream in a bowl.
- Shape the mixture into 1x3-inch rolls.
- Place the sausage rolls on the tenderloin pieces; roll up. Wrap the tenderloin rolls with the bacon strips and fasten with wooden picks.
- Brown the rolls evenly in the 1/4 cup margarine in a skillet. Add the water.
- Fry gently for 30 minutes, turning frequently; remove the rolls from the skillet and set aside.
- Sauté the mushrooms and onion in the remaining 2 tablespoons margarine in a small skillet.
- Serve over the tenderloin rolls.

GRILLED PORK TENDERLOIN WITH MUSTARD SAUCE

1 (2½- to 3-pound) pork tenderloin
¼ cup soy sauce
¼ cup bourbon
2 tablespoons brown sugar
Mustard Sauce

Yield: 4 to 6 servings

- Place the pork in a mixture of soy sauce, bourbon and brown sugar in a container.
- Marinate, covered, in the refrigerator for 3 to 4 hours.
- Grill the tenderloin for 12 to 15 minutes per side or until cooked through, basting occasionally with the marinade.
- Slice the tenderloin diagonally.
- Serve the Mustard Sauce with the tenderloin.

MUSTARD SAUCE

⅓ cup mayonnaise
⅓ cup sour cream
1 teaspoon dry mustard
1½ teaspoons vinegar
Salt to taste
1 tablespoon finely chopped scallions

- Combine the mayonnaise, sour cream, dry mustard, vinegar, salt and scallions in a bowl; mix well.

Tom Nienhuis's Pork Scallops with Pears and Curry

3 pork tenderloins
Seasoned flour
2 tablespoons olive oil
2 tablespoons brandy
1 cup chicken stock
1 cup light cream
4 pears, cut into halves
1 tablespoon curry powder

Yield: 8 servings

- Trim the tenderloins and cut each into 8 sections.
- Pound the pork into scallops; dredge in seasoned flour.
- Sauté the scallops in the oil in a skillet a few at a time until cooked through; do not crowd the skillet.
- Place in a baking dish.
- Heat in a 400-degree oven for 3 to 4 minutes.
- Remove the skillet from heat.
- Add the brandy, stirring to deglaze the skillet.
- Return to heat.
- Cook until most of the liquid is absorbed.
- Add the chicken stock and cream.
- Cook until thickened, stirring frequently.
- Add the pears and curry powder.
- Cook until the pears are tender.
- Spoon over the pork scallops.

Apricot Pork Chops

1 tablespoon butter
1 pound boneless pork chops
1 teaspoon butter
¹/₂ cup apricot jam
2 green onions, sliced
¹/₄ teaspoon dry mustard
1 tablespoon cider vinegar

Yield: 4 to 6 servings

- Heat the 1 tablespoon butter in a skillet over medium-high heat.
- Add the pork chops.
- Sauté the pork chops for 5 minutes per side or until cooked through; remove from the skillet.
- Add 1 teaspoon butter, jam, green onions, dry mustard and vinegar to the skillet; mix well.
- Simmer, covered, for 3 to 4 minutes or until heated through.
- Add the pork chops.
- Cook until the pork chops are heated through.
- Serve the pan drippings over the pork chops.

Honey-Glazed Pork Chops

6 center-cut pork chops
¹/₂ cup honey
3 tablespoons cider vinegar
1 teaspoon salt
¹/₄ teaspoon dry mustard
1 large apple, peeled, sliced
¹/₄ cup raisins
2 tablespoons brown sugar

Yield: 4 to 6 servings

- Place the pork chops in a baking dish.
- Pour a mixture of the honey, vinegar, salt and dry mustard over the chops.
- Top with the apple and raisins.
- Sprinkle with the brown sugar.
- Bake at 325 degrees for 1 hour, basting occasionally with the pan juices.

Sandpiper Pork Chops with Arugula, Goat Cheese and Tomato

These are wonderful, and they're even better with the view the Sandpiper Restaurant offers.

4 (16-ounce) double-thickness
   center-cut pork chops
Salt and pepper to taste
1 tablespoon olive oil
¼ cup goat cheese
¼ cup slivered basil
1 cup slivered arugula
3 Roma tomatoes, chopped into
   ¼-inch pieces
¼ cup olive oil
2 tablespoons balsamic vinegar

Yield: 4 servings

- Sprinkle the pork chops with salt and pepper.
- Brown in the 1 tablespoon oil in a skillet.
- Remove the chops to a baking dish.
- Bake, covered, at 375 degrees for 20 minutes or until cooked through.
- Spread each chop with 1 tablespoon of the goat cheese; sprinkle with the basil and arugula.
- Top with the tomatoes.
- Bake for 4 minutes longer.
- Remove the chops to individual serving plates.
- Whisk ¼ cup olive oil and vinegar in a bowl.
- Season with salt and pepper.
- Drizzle the mixture over and around each chop.

Pork Chops Topped with Spinach and Mushrooms

A favorite way to cook pork chops—they're really tender.

1 tablespoon butter

4 to 6 (³/₄-inch thick) boneless pork chops

1 cup finely chopped mushrooms

1 tablespoon butter

¹/₂ cup thawed frozen chopped spinach

¹/₃ cup finely chopped red onion

1 egg

1 teaspoon salt

¹/₈ teaspoon pepper

3 tablespoons shredded Cheddar cheese

Yield: 4 servings

- Heat the 1 tablespoon butter in a skillet and add the pork chops.
- Brown the chops quickly to seal in the juices.
- Remove the chops to an ovenproof dish.
- Sauté the mushrooms in 1 tablespoon butter in a skillet until the mushrooms are no longer moist; let stand to cool.
- Combine the mushrooms, spinach, onion, egg, salt and pepper in a bowl and mix well.
- Spoon the mixture over the pork chops.
- Bake at 350 degrees for 30 minutes.
- Sprinkle with the cheese.
- Bake for 10 minutes longer or until the chops are cooked through and the juices run clear when pierced with a fork.
- Serve with a salad or sliced herbed tomatoes and rice or boiled new potatoes.

Weekend Spareribs

3 pounds country-style spareribs

1½ cups catsup

¼ cup Worcestershire sauce

⅓ cup red wine vinegar

¼ cup packed brown sugar

2 teaspoons salt

½ teaspoon garlic salt

¼ teaspoon pepper

Yield: 8 to 12 servings

- Combine the spareribs with enough water to cover in a large saucepan. Boil for 1½ to 2 hours or until tender.
- Place the ribs in a 9x13-inch baking pan.
- Pour a mixture of the catsup, Worcestershire sauce, vinegar, brown sugar, salt, garlic salt and pepper over the ribs. Marinate, covered, in the refrigerator for several hours.
- Bake at 350 degrees for 45 minutes.

Chicken Florentine

4 to 6 boneless skinless chicken breasts

1 tablespoon butter

3 tablespoons flour

¾ cup chicken stock

½ cup milk

¼ teaspoon salt

⅛ teaspoon each garlic powder and pepper

½ teaspoon curry powder

½ cup each cold water, nonfat mayonnaise and brown rice

1 (10-ounce) package frozen spinach, thawed

⅓ cup grated Parmesan cheese

Yield: 4 to 6 servings

- Rinse the chicken and pat dry.
- Melt the butter in a saucepan. Add the flour, chicken stock and milk. Bring to a boil, stirring constantly.
- Add the salt, garlic powder, pepper and curry powder. Cook for 1 minute; remove from heat. Stir in the water and mayonnaise.
- Sprinkle the rice in a 7x11-inch baking pan.
- Layer the spinach, half the flour mixture and the chicken over the rice. Pour the remaining flour mixture over the chicken. Sprinkle with the cheese.
- Bake at 350 degrees for 1 hour.

Honey Chicken

This is easy and delicious.

6 chicken breasts
$^1/_4$ cup butter
$^1/_2$ cup honey
$^1/_4$ cup yellow mustard
1 teaspoon curry powder

Yield: 6 servings

- Rinse the chicken and pat dry.
- Melt the butter in a shallow baking pan.
- Stir in the honey, mustard and curry powder.
- Roll the chicken in the mixture.
- Arrange the chicken meaty side up in a single layer in the pan.
- Bake at 375 degrees for 1 hour.

Easy Orange Chicken

8 boneless chicken breasts
$^1/_3$ cup butter
1 (12-ounce) can frozen orange juice concentrate, thawed
1 envelope onion soup mix

Yield: 8 servings

- Rinse the chicken and pat dry.
- Melt the butter in a large skillet.
- Brown the chicken in the melted butter.
- Place the chicken in a shallow baking dish.
- Pour a mixture of the orange juice concentrate and soup mix over the chicken.
- Bake at 325 degrees for 45 minutes.

Taos Chicken Cordon Bleu

A classic recipe spiced up with some South-of-the-Border flair.

4 skinless boneless chicken breasts
8 slices ham
8 slices Swiss cheese
1/2 cup salsa
1/4 cup guacamole
1/4 cup chopped green chiles
1/4 cup sour cream
2 black olives, cut into halves

Yield: 4 servings

- Rinse the chicken and pat dry.
- Grill or broil the chicken until cooked through.
- Arrange the chicken on a flat baking sheet.
- Top each piece of chicken with 2 slices ham and 2 slices cheese.
- Bake at 350 degrees for 5 minutes.
- Spoon 1/4 of the salsa into the center of each of 4 individual serving plates.
- Top each with guacamole; sprinkle with the green chiles.
- Arrange the baked chicken on the serving plates; top each piece with 1 tablespoon sour cream.
- Top each with an olive half.

CURRY CHICKEN

This makes a fun, unique meal.

3 tablespoons melted butter

¼ cup chopped onion

1½ teaspoons curry powder

3 tablespoons flour

¾ teaspoon salt

¾ teaspoon sugar

⅛ teaspoon ginger

1 cup chicken broth

1 cup milk

2 cups chopped cooked chicken

Yield: 4 servings

- Mix the melted butter, onion and curry powder in a saucepan or skillet.
- Blend in the flour, salt, sugar and ginger.
- Cook over medium heat until the mixture is smooth, stirring constantly; reduce the heat to low.
- Stir in the broth and milk. Bring to a boil.
- Simmer for 1 minute.
- Add the chicken.
- Cook until heated through.
- Serve over hot cooked rice and have the guests choose their own toppings.
- Suggested toppings include flaked coconut, cashews, pineapple, golden raisins, chopped green onions and sunflower kernels.

Down-Home Chicken Pie

1 package all ready pie pastries
1/2 cup chopped onion
1/4 cup margarine
1/2 cup flour
3 cups chicken broth
2 cups chopped cooked chicken
1 cup cooked sliced carrots
1/2 cup sliced fresh mushrooms
2 cups chopped cooked potatoes
1/2 cup frozen peas, thawed
1/2 teaspoon salt
1/4 teaspoon pepper

Yield: 2 to 4 servings

- Fit 1 pastry into a pie plate.
- Cook the onion in the margarine in a skillet until the onion is tender.
- Add the flour.
- Cook for 1 to 2 minutes or until heated through, stirring constantly.
- Whisk in the broth slowly.
- Cook until the mixture is thickened and smooth, stirring constantly.
- Add the chicken, carrots, mushrooms, potatoes, peas, salt and pepper; mix well.
- Pour the mixture into the pastry-lined pie plate.
- Top with the remaining pastry, sealing and fluting the edge and cutting vents.
- Bake at 400 degrees for 1 hour or until browned.

Elegant Chicken Potpie

1 package frozen puff pastry, thawed

2 pounds boneless skinless chicken breasts and thighs

1 dried bay leaf

4 to 5 whole peppercorns

3 tablespoons melted butter

2 tablespoons flour

1 cup whipping cream

1/2 teaspoon dried tarragon

1/2 teaspoon Tabasco sauce, or to taste

Salt and pepper to taste

1/2 cup peeled pearl onions

1 cup small peas

1 egg, beaten

Yield: 4 servings

- Roll the pastry to fit across the top of a 1½-quart baking dish, allowing a 1½-inch overlap; cut leaf shapes from the leftover pastry pieces. Freeze between 2 sheets of waxed paper.

- Rinse the chicken. Combine the chicken, bay leaf and peppercorns with water to cover in a skillet. Poach for 15 to 20 minutes or until cooked through. Cool.

- Remove the chicken, reserving and straining 1 cup of the poaching liquid. Cut the chicken into small chunks.

- Blend the butter and flour in a large saucepan. Cook over medium heat for several minutes, stirring frequently. Stir in reserved liquid gradually.

- Cook until thickened, stirring constantly; remove from heat and cool slightly. Add the cream, tarragon, Tabasco sauce, salt and pepper; mix well.

- Combine the chicken, onions and peas in a 1½-quart baking dish. Pour the sauce over the top; cool completely.

- Brush the top of the pastry with some of the beaten egg. Place the pastry on top of baking dish, not touching the sauce. Arrange the leaves on top of the pastry, securing with the remaining egg.

- Bake at 450 degrees for 12 to 15 minutes. Reduce the oven temperature to 350 degrees. Bake for 35 minutes longer or until golden brown and puffed.

- Loosen the crust with a sharp knife. Lift off and set aside. Spoon the filling onto serving plates and top each with crust.

Thai Chicken and Vegetables

1½ pounds chicken breasts, skinned, boned, cut into 1-inch pieces

2 tablespoons vegetable oil

1 teaspoon five-spice powder

½ to 1½ teaspoons salt

½ teaspoon MSG (optional)

½ teaspoon garlic powder

½ teaspoon ginger

½ teaspoon black pepper

½ teaspoon cayenne

1 tablespoon soy sauce

1 cup chicken broth

1 tablespoon curry powder

2 tablespoons rice wine vinegar or vinegar

1 (14-ounce) can coconut milk

1 (16-ounce) package frozen mixed broccoli, carrots, water chestnuts and red peppers

5 cups hot cooked rice

Yield: 6 to 8 servings

- Rinse the chicken and pat dry.
- Heat the oil in a large skillet over medium-high heat.
- Stir in the five-spice powder, salt, garlic powder, ginger, black pepper, cayenne and soy sauce; blend well.
- Add the chicken.
- Sauté for 5 to 8 minutes or until the chicken is coated, lightly browned and cooked through.
- Add the chicken broth, curry powder, vinegar and coconut milk; mix well.
- Bring to a boil; reduce the heat.
- Simmer for 20 to 25 minutes or until the chicken is cooked through, stirring occasionally.
- Add the frozen vegetables. Bring to a boil.
- Cook for 3 to 5 minutes longer or until the vegetables are tender-crisp.
- Serve over the rice.
- Do not substitute cream of coconut for coconut milk in this recipe.

Marinated Chicken Wings

This also makes a great appetizer.

2 to 3 pounds chicken wings

1 cup soy sauce

1 tablespoon sugar or ¼ cup pineapple
   juice

¼ cup white wine

2 cloves of garlic, minced

¼ cup vegetable oil

1 teaspoon ginger

Yield: 6 to 8 servings

- Rinse the chicken and pat dry.
- Cut the tips from the chicken wings and discard
  the tips.
- Combine the soy sauce, sugar, wine, garlic, oil and
  ginger in a large bowl; mix well.
- Add the chicken.
- Marinate in the refrigerator for 6 to 10 hours.
- Place the chicken in a baking dish.
- Bake at 350 degrees for 1½ to 2 hours or until cooked
  through, basting occasionally with the marinade.

Turkey Tenderloin

1 pound turkey tenderloin

¼ cup soy sauce

¼ cup vegetable oil

¼ cup dry sherry

2 tablespoons lemon juice

2 tablespoons dried onion

⅓ teaspoon ginger

⅛ teaspoon pepper, or to taste

⅛ teaspoon garlic salt, or to taste

Yield: 4 servings

- Rinse the turkey.
- Mix the soy sauce, oil, sherry, lemon juice, onion,
  ginger, pepper and garlic salt in a shallow pan.
- Add the turkey, turning to coat both sides.
- Marinate, covered, in the refrigerator for several
  hours, turning occasionally.
- Grill the turkey over hot coals for 6 to 8 minutes
  per side or until cooked through.
- Turkey steaks are done when there is no pink in the
  center; do not overcook.

Chinese Steamed Fish

6 green onions

2 pounds fresh trout, striped bass or
snapper fillets

2 teaspoons salt

2 tablespoons peeled fresh ginger, cut
into 1½-inch shreds

2 tablespoons soy sauce

2 tablespoons peanut oil

1 slice fresh ginger

Crushed white pepper to taste

Yield: 4 to 6 servings

- Cut 2 whole green onions into 2-inch lengths; cut
  the green part only of the remaining 4 green onions
  into 1½-inch shreds, reserving the white part for
  another use.
- Rinse the fish and dry it thoroughly.
- Make several diagonal cuts across both sides of
  each fillet.
- Rub the fillets inside and out with salt.
- Scatter the green onion lengths in a bamboo Chinese
  steamer; top with the fish.
- Scatter half the green onion shreds and 1 tablespoon
  of the ginger shreds over the fish.
- Cover the steamer and place it in a wok. Add water to
  the wok; do not allow to touch the steamer.
- Steam the fish over medium-high heat for 10 minutes
  per inch of thickness or until opaque.
- Warm the soy sauce in a medium saucepan for 30
  seconds or until fragrant.
- Heat the peanut oil and ginger slice in a small
  saucepan until very hot and almost smoking.
- Remove the fish to a serving platter.
- Sprinkle the pepper over the fish; pour the soy sauce
  over the fish.
- Sprinkle with the remaining green onion shreds and
  ginger shreds.
- Pour the hot oil over the fish; it should sizzle.
- Serve with hot cooked rice and steamed broccoli.

GRILLED SALMON WITH TARRAGON MAYONNAISE

8 (4- to 6-ounce) salmon steaks
Tarragon Mayonnaise

Yield: 8 servings

- Preheat the coals or the broiler.
- Place the grill rack 5 inches from the heat source; brush the grill rack with vegetable oil.
- Place the salmon on the grill rack and spread each steak with 2½ tablespoons of the Tarragon Mayonnaise mixture.
- Broil for 6 minutes.
- Turn the salmon over and brush each steak with 2½ tablespoons of the Mayonnaise.
- Broil until the salmon flakes easily and is barely opaque.
- Arrange the salmon on a serving platter.
- Garnish with halved lemon and lime slices and sprigs of fresh tarragon and parsley.
- May substitute ½ cup chopped fresh parsley plus 2 teaspoons crumbled dried tarragon for the fresh tarragon.

TARRAGON MAYONNAISE

2 cups mayonnaise
¼ cup chopped fresh tarragon
3 tablespoons minced green onions or red onion
2 tablespoons fresh lemon juice
2 tablespoons chopped capers
¼ teaspoon freshly ground pepper
Salt to taste

- Blend the mayonnaise, tarragon, green onions, lemon juice, capers and pepper in a large bowl; season with salt.
- Chill, covered, for 2 to 24 hours.

Teriyaki Grilled Salmon Steaks

1/3 cup soy sauce

2 tablespoons dry sherry

1 tablespoon sesame oil

1 tablespoon grated fresh ginger

1 clove of garlic, minced

1/2 teaspoon pepper

4 (1-inch-thick) salmon steaks

Yield: 4 servings

- Mix the soy sauce, sherry, sesame oil, ginger, garlic and pepper in a large bowl.
- Add the salmon.
- Marinate at room temperature for 30 minutes or in the refrigerator for 2 hours, turning frequently.
- Place the salmon on a well oiled grill or in a lightly oiled broiling pan.
- Grill or broil for 4 to 5 minutes per side or until the salmon is slightly firm and opaque.

Grilled Swordfish

1 small onion

2 tablespoons fresh lemon juice

2 teaspoons olive oil

1 teaspoon salt

1/2 teaspoon freshly ground pepper

1 1/2 pounds swordfish steaks

2 tablespoons fresh lemon juice

2 teaspoons olive oil

Yield: 4 servings

- Cut the onion into 1/4-inch slices and separate into rings.
- Mix the onion, 2 tablespoons lemon juice, 2 teaspoons olive oil, salt and pepper in a deep bowl.
- Add the swordfish, turning to coat.
- Marinate in the refrigerator for 4 hours, turning occasionally.
- Grill the swordfish until the fish flakes easily, brushing occasionally with a mixture of 2 tablespoons lemon juice and 2 teaspoons olive oil.

CALYPSO'S SWORDFISH WITH PINEAPPLE SALSA

*T*odd Van Wieren, executive chef at Calypso's Restaurant, makes swordfish festive with this culinary masterpiece.

6 (6- to 8-ounce) swordfish steaks
3 tablespoons lemon juice
3 tablespoons olive oil
Salt and pepper to taste
Pineapple Salsa

Yield: 6 servings

- Brush the swordfish with a mixture of the lemon juice and 3 tablespoons olive oil; season with salt and pepper to taste.
- Broil on a rack in a broiler pan until the fish flakes easily, turning once.
- Place the swordfish steaks on individual serving plates.
- Top with the Pineapple Salsa.

PINEAPPLE SALSA

1 pineapple, peeled, cut into ¼-inch cubes
1 medium red onion, chopped
1 medium red bell pepper, chopped
1 medium green bell pepper, chopped
1 serrano chile, chopped
¼ cup olive oil
2 tablespoons lime juice
1 tablespoon cilantro
1 tablespoon parsley
1 teaspoon salt
1 teaspoon pepper

- Broil the pineapple on a rack in a broiler pan just until browned.
- Combine the pineapple, onion, bell peppers, chile, ¼ cup olive oil, lime juice, cilantro, parsley, 1 teaspoon salt and 1 teaspoon pepper in a large bowl.
- Chill the salsa thoroughly.
- May add additional chiles for a hotter salsa; the salsa may also be served as an appetizer with tortilla chips.

Tom Gebben's Pan-Fried Brook Trout in an Almond and Sage Crust

Chef Tom Gebben suggests serving this dish with boiled new potatoes and steamed asparagus spears.

1/2 cup flour

1/4 cup toasted sliced almonds

3 tablespoons chopped fresh sage leaves

1/2 teaspoon salt

Freshly cracked pepper to taste

2 whole trout, cleaned, cut into fillets

1/4 cup peanut oil

Yield: 2 servings

- Combine the flour, almonds, sage, salt and pepper in a bowl.
- Spread the mixture on a baking sheet or a large plate.
- Place the fish meaty side down on the flour mixture.
- Let the fish stand for 2 to 4 minutes; shake off the excess flour mixture and lightly coat the other side of the fish with the flour mixture.
- Heat the oil in a skillet. Add the trout.
- Fry for 5 minutes or until golden and crisp; turn the trout over.
- Cook for 5 minutes longer or until the trout tests done.
- Garnish with lemon wedges.

Zesty Grilled Tuna

This is perfect for those who don't like their fish too "fishy."

3 tablespoons soy sauce

3 tablespoons orange juice

1 tablespoon vegetable oil

2 tablespoons catsup

3/4 teaspoon chopped fresh parsley

1/2 shallot, chopped

1 clove of garlic, minced

1 teaspoon lemon juice

1/2 teaspoon oregano

1/2 teaspoon pepper

1 pound tuna or swordfish fillets

Yield: 4 servings

- Combine the soy sauce, orange juice, oil, catsup, parsley, shallot, garlic, lemon juice, oregano and pepper in a large bowl; mix well.
- Add the fish.
- Marinate at room temperature for 1 hour.
- Grill until the fish tests done.

CRAB AND ZUCCHINI CASSEROLE

2 medium zucchini, sliced

1/2 cup chopped onion

2 cloves of garlic, minced

1/2 cup butter or margarine

1/8 teaspoon pepper

1 teaspoon basil

1 pound crab meat

1 1/2 cups shredded Cheddar cheese

1 cup seasoned bread crumbs

3 medium tomatoes, chopped

Yield: 4 to 6 servings

- Sauté the zucchini, onion and garlic in the butter in a skillet for 5 minutes or until the vegetables are tender.
- Combine the vegetables with the pepper, basil, crab meat, cheese and bread crumbs in a large bowl; mix well.
- Add the tomatoes and toss lightly.
- Spoon into a glass baking dish.
- Bake at 375 degrees for 30 to 35 minutes or until heated through.

Shrimp Scampi

2 cloves of garlic, minced

1 bunch green onions, chopped

2 tablespoons butter

1 tablespoon olive oil

1 cup chicken broth

1/2 cup lemon juice

1 bay leaf

1/4 cup parsley

1/4 cup basil

1/2 cup clam juice

1 pound large shrimp, peeled,
   deveined, sliced lengthwise

1 large tomato, chopped

1 pound linguini, cooked

1/4 to 1/2 cup grated Parmesan cheese

Yield: 4 to 6 servings

- Sauté the garlic and green onions in the butter and olive oil in a large skillet.
- Add the broth, lemon juice, bay leaf, parsley, basil and clam juice.
- Bring to a boil; reduce the heat. Simmer over low heat for several minutes.
- Add the shrimp. Cook until the shrimp turn pink.
- Stir in the tomato. Simmer for 5 minutes longer; remove the bay leaf.
- Serve over the linguini, sprinkled with the cheese.

Shrimp Stroganoff

2 tablespoons butter or margarine

2 tablespoons finely chopped onion

8 ounces fresh shrimp, peeled, deveined

1 (10-ounce) can cream of shrimp soup

1/2 cup skim milk

1/2 cup low-fat sour cream

1/4 teaspoon paprika, or to taste

Salt and pepper to taste

8 ounces egg fettuccini, cooked

Yield: 4 to 6 servings

- Melt the butter in a skillet. Add the onion.
- Sauté until the onion is tender.
- Add the shrimp. Cook until the shrimp turn pink.
- Blend in the soup and skim milk.
- Cook until heated through; do not boil.
- Stir in the sour cream and paprika.
- Season with salt and pepper.
- Serve over the hot fettuccini.

Cavatini

2 pounds ground beef
1 green bell pepper, chopped
1 large onion, chopped
8 ounces fresh mushrooms, sliced
4 to 6 ounces pepperoni
2 envelopes spaghetti sauce mix
1 (12-ounce) can tomato paste
3 (12-ounce) cans water
1 cup shell pasta, cooked
1 cup twist pasta, cooked
1 cup ziti, cooked
2 cups shredded mozzarella cheese
Grated Parmesan cheese to taste

Yield: 8 to 10 servings

- Brown the ground beef in a skillet.
- Add the green pepper and onion.
- Sauté until the vegetables are tender; drain.
- Add the mushrooms, pepperoni, spaghetti sauce mix, tomato paste and water; mix well.
- Simmer over low heat for 1 hour.
- Add the cooked pasta; mix well.
- Spoon the mixture into a nonstick 9x13-inch baking pan.
- Top with the mozzarella cheese; sprinkle with the Parmesan cheese.
- Bake at 350 degrees for 25 to 30 minutes or until bubbly and heated through.

South-of-the-Border Lasagna

1 pound ground beef
2 (14-ounce) cans tomato sauce
2 envelopes taco seasoning mix
1 (4-ounce) can chopped green chiles
4 flour tortillas
1 cup shredded Monterey Jack cheese
1 cup shredded Cheddar cheese

Yield: 6 servings

- Brown the ground beef in a skillet; drain and set aside.
- Bring the tomato sauce and seasoning mix to a boil in a medium saucepan; reduce the heat.
- Simmer for 10 minutes; remove from heat.
- Remove and reserve 1 cup of the mixture.
- Add the ground beef and green chiles to the remaining mixture; mix well.
- Place 1 tortilla in a round baking pan or casserole dish sprayed with nonstick cooking spray.
- Cover with 1/3 of the ground beef mixture and 1/4 of each cheese.
- Repeat the layers twice.
- Top with the remaining tortilla.
- Pour the reserved sauce over the top.
- Sprinkle with the remaining cheeses.
- Bake at 350 degrees for 40 minutes.
- Let stand for 5 minutes before serving.
- Cut into wedges to serve.

Spaghetti Bolognese

1 (28-ounce) can tomatoes
2 tablespoons olive oil
1 onion, chopped
1 pound lean ground beef
½ carrot, finely chopped
½ stalk celery, finely chopped
1 cup dry white wine
⅛ teaspoon nutmeg
½ cup milk
1 cup beef broth
1 teaspoon salt
Pepper to taste
1 teaspoon basil
⅛ teaspoon thyme
1 bay leaf
1 pound spaghetti, cooked
1 cup grated Parmesan cheese

Yield: 4 to 6 servings

- Press the undrained tomatoes through a sieve into a bowl; discard the seeds, reserving the tomatoes and juice.
- Heat the olive oil in a skillet. Add the onion. Sauté until tender.
- Add the ground beef.
- Brown the ground beef, stirring until crumbly; drain.
- Stir in the carrot and celery.
- Cook over medium-high heat for 2 minutes.
- Add the wine. Cook for 4 to 6 minutes or until the wine has evaporated.
- Stir in the nutmeg and milk.
- Cook over medium heat for 3 to 4 minutes or until the milk has evaporated; remove from the heat.
- Stir in the reserved tomatoes and juice, beef broth, salt, pepper, basil, thyme and bay leaf.
- Bring to a boil; reduce the heat to low.
- Simmer for 1½ hours or until the liquid has evaporated, stirring frequently.
- Remove the bay leaf.
- Serve the sauce over the hot spaghetti.
- Sprinkle with the cheese.

Chef Tom Nienhuis's Pasta with Sausage and Sauerkraut

8 ounces sausage

1 pound pasta

8 ounces sauerkraut, drained

2 tablespoons butter

1 teaspoon red pepper flakes

1/2 cup shredded Swiss cheese
(optional)

Yield: 4 to 6 servings

- Cook the sausage in a skillet; drain and chop.
- Cook the pasta using the package directions; drain and blanch.
- Sauté the sauerkraut in the butter in a large skillet for 5 minutes.
- Add the sausage, pasta and pepper flakes.
- Cook until heated through.
- Stir in the cheese, if desired.

Pasta with Red Sauce

Preparing this sauce is almost as easy as serving bottled sauce, and it tastes much better.

8 to 12 Italian sausages
1 (28-ounce) can tomatoes
2 (28-ounce) cans tomato sauce
1 (12-ounce) can tomato paste
1 tablespoon parsley
1 tablespoon garlic salt
1 tablespoon oregano
1 teaspoon minced garlic
1/4 cup grated Parmesan cheese
1 green bell pepper, cut into quarters
1 onion, cut into halves
2 pounds pasta

Yield: 8 to 12 servings

- Cut slits in the sausages and combine with enough water to cover in a skillet.
- Cook until the sausages are cooked through; drain the skillet, reserving a small amount of the pan drippings.
- Chop the tomatoes in a blender.
- Combine the tomatoes, tomato sauce and tomato paste in a large saucepan.
- Add the parsley, garlic salt, oregano, garlic and cheese; mix well.
- Add the sausages and reserved pan drippings.
- Stir in the green pepper and onion.
- Bring to a boil over medium heat.
- Simmer for 1 1/2 hours or until the sauce is of the desired consistency.
- Cook the pasta using the package directions.
- Serve the sauce over the pasta, making sure each serving includes a sausage.
- Use any leftover sauce for pizza or lasagna.

CHICKEN AND SUN-DRIED TOMATO FETTUCCINI

Just sit back and enjoy the compliments.

1¹/₂ boneless skinless chicken breasts,
    cut into 1-inch strips

1 cup finely chopped zucchini

2 tablespoons olive oil

1 cup oil-pack sun-dried tomato
    halves, blanched, cut into strips

1 tablespoon capers, rinsed, chopped

1 to 3 anchovy fillets (optional)

1¹/₂ pounds fettuccini, cooked, drained

1 to 2 cups whipping cream

Yield: 12 to 15 servings

- Sauté the chicken and zucchini in the olive oil in a skillet.
- Add the tomatoes, capers, anchovies and pasta.
- Cook until the flavors are blended and the pasta is warm.
- Add the whipping cream.
- Cook until heated through; do not allow the liquid to reduce by much.

Pasta with Fresh Greens and Roasted Garlic

6 to 8 thin cloves of garlic

1 teaspoon olive oil

1 pound penne or ziti

1 tablespoon olive oil

1 red onion, thinly sliced

1 yellow bell pepper, cut into long thin slices

2 green onions, diagonally sliced

1/4 teaspoon red bell pepper

Salt to taste

2 bunches escarole or broccoli rabe, trimmed, cut into 1-inch ribbons

12 cherry tomatoes, cut into halves

1/8 teaspoon nutmeg, or to taste

Freshly ground basil to taste

1 to 2 cups cooked chicken strips (optional)

Yield: 4 to 6 servings

- Place the garlic in 1 teaspoon olive oil in a small baking pan.
- Bake at 375 degrees for 12 to 15 minutes or until tender.
- Peel the cooled garlic and cut the cloves into halves lengthwise.
- Boil the pasta in enough water to cover in a saucepan for 6 to 8 minutes or until partially cooked.
- Heat 1 tablespoon olive oil in a large skillet over medium-high heat.
- Add the onion, bell pepper, green onions, red pepper and salt.
- Cook until the onion is tender-crisp, tossing frequently. Add the garlic.
- Cook for 1 minute longer. Add the escarole to the partially cooked pasta.
- Cook for 5 minutes or just until the pasta and escarole are tender; drain, reserving 1 cup of the cooking liquid.
- Return the pasta and escarole to the saucepan over low heat.
- Add the green onion mixture, tomatoes, nutmeg and basil. Add the chicken.
- Cook until heated through, adding enough of the reserved cooking liquid to moisten.
- Garnish with freshly grated Parmesan cheese.

Linguini with Scallops

1 teaspoon margarine

1 teaspoon olive oil

1 pound fresh or thawed frozen
   scallops

1½ cups chicken broth

¾ cup dry white wine

3 tablespoons lemon juice

¾ cup chopped green onions

½ cup chopped fresh parsley

2 tablespoons capers, drained

1 teaspoon dillweed

½ teaspoon pepper

12 ounces linguini, cooked

Yield: 4 servings

- Melt the margarine in a large skillet.
- Add the olive oil and scallops.
- Cook for 2 minutes; remove the scallops and set aside.
- Stir the broth, wine and lemon juice into the skillet.
- Boil for 10 minutes.
- Stir in the green onions, parsley, capers, dillweed and pepper; reduce the heat.
- Simmer for 1 minute.
- Add the scallops. Cook until heated through.
- Pour over the linguini and toss gently.

Auburn Restaurant's Sauteed Shrimp and Linguini

2 tablespoons olive oil

⅓ cup chopped onion

⅓ cup finely chopped carrot

⅓ cup chopped celery

4 teaspoons minced garlic

6 tablespoons flour

2½ pounds fresh tomatoes, chopped

1 to 2 cups low-sodium chicken broth

1 cup dry white wine

2¼ teaspoons dried basil

¼ teaspoon dried crushed red pepper

1 (14-ounce) can artichoke hearts, chopped

½ cup chopped sun-dried tomatoes

2 to 4 cups whipping cream

2¼ pounds large shrimp, peeled, deveined

Salt and black pepper to taste

1½ pounds linguini, cooked, drained

6 tablespoons fresh basil leaves

¾ cup grated Parmesan cheese

Yield: 6 to 8 servings

- Heat the olive oil in a heavy skillet or stockpot over medium-high heat.
- Add the onion, carrot and celery.
- Sauté for 2 minutes. Add the garlic. Sauté for 1 minute longer.
- Sprinkle the flour over the vegetables.
- Cook for 2 minutes, stirring constantly.
- Stir in the fresh tomatoes, broth, wine, basil and red pepper.
- Bring to a boil; reduce the heat to medium.
- Cook until of a thin sauce consistency, stirring frequently.
- Add the artichoke hearts and sun-dried tomatoes.
- Cook for 8 minutes or until the artichoke hearts are tender, stirring occasionally; drain any remaining liquid.
- Add the whipping cream. Simmer for 1 to 2 minutes.
- Add the shrimp.
- Simmer for 5 minutes or until the shrimp turn pink and the whipping cream is reduced.
- Season with salt and black pepper.
- Pour over the linguini, tossing to coat. Remove to a serving bowl or individual plates.
- Sprinkle with the fresh basil and cheese.

Tri-Colored Fusilli with Shrimp and Roasted Peppers

1 large red bell pepper

1 large green bell pepper

12 ounces mixed egg, spinach and tomato fusilli

Salt and pepper to taste

1/2 cup white wine vinegar

1 tablespoon Dijon mustard

1/2 cup olive oil

8 ounces peeled cooked shrimp

2 to 3 tablespoons chopped fresh basil

Yield: 3 to 4 servings

- Char the bell peppers in a broiler or over an open flame until the skin blackens, turning as necessary.
- Place the peppers in a sealable plastic bag and steam for 10 minutes.
- Remove the skins and seeds; rinse and pat dry.
- Cut the peppers into fusilli-size strips.
- Cook the fusilli in a large pot of rapidly boiling water; drain.
- Season with salt and pepper.
- Blend the vinegar, Dijon mustard, salt and pepper in a bowl.
- Whisk in the olive oil in a thin stream.
- Add the peppers, fusilli, shrimp and basil; toss well.
- Serve at room temperature or chilled.

Angel Hair Pasta with Pine Nuts, Basil and Tomatoes

This is a pasta lover's dream.

¹/₄ cup olive oil

¹/₂ cup pine nuts

4 large cloves of garlic, minced

3 tomatoes, chopped

2 (6-ounce) jars marinated artichoke hearts, drained

¹/₄ cup chopped fresh basil

2 teaspoons fresh oregano

Salt and pepper to taste

9 ounces fresh angel hair pasta, cooked, drained

Grated Parmesan cheese to taste

Yield: 3 to 4 servings

- Heat the oil in a skillet over medium heat. Add the pine nuts and garlic.
- Sauté for 5 minutes or until golden brown.
- Stir in the tomatoes, artichoke hearts, basil and oregano. Cook until heated through.
- Season with salt and pepper.
- Pour the sauce over the pasta and toss.
- Sprinkle with Parmesan cheese.

Pasta with Cauliflower in Spicy Pink Sauce

3 cups tomato purée

1¹/₂ cups whipping cream

¹/₂ cup freshly grated Romano cheese

¹/₂ cup coarsely shredded fontina cheese

2 tablespoons ricotta cheese

1 teaspoon crushed red pepper

1 teaspoon kosher salt

Salt to taste

5 quarts water

1 head cauliflower, coarsely chopped

1 pound penne

3 tablespoons unsalted butter

Yield: 6 to 8 servings

- Mix the tomato purée, whipping cream, Romano cheese, fontina cheese, ricotta cheese, pepper and kosher salt in a bowl; set aside.
- Bring salted water to a boil in a large saucepan.
- Add the cauliflower and pasta.
- Cook for 5 minutes; drain.
- Add the pasta mixture to the cheese mixture, tossing to combine.
- Spoon into a baking dish or 6 to 8 individual shallow ceramic baking dishes.
- Top with the butter.
- Bake at 500 degrees for 7 to 10 minutes or until bubbly and browned.

Greek Spaghetti

1 pound spaghetti
2 tablespoons (about) olive oil
6 to 10 cloves of garlic, minced
Pepper and garlic pepper to taste
8 ounces feta cheese

Yield: 4 to 6 servings

- Boil the spaghetti in enough water to cover until al dente; drain.
- Coat a large skillet with the olive oil. Add the spaghetti and garlic. Sauté for 8 minutes.
- Add the pepper, garlic pepper and 2 ounces of the cheese. Cook until the cheese melts, tossing constantly.
- Remove the spaghetti to a bowl.
- Crumble the remaining cheese into the spaghetti and toss well.

Pasta Pesto Florentine

2 to 3 cloves of garlic
1/2 cup walnuts (optional)
1 (10-ounce) package frozen chopped spinach, thawed, drained
1/2 cup grated Parmesan cheese
1/2 cup olive oil
1/3 cup water
1 teaspoon salt
1 teaspoon dried basil
1 large tomato, chopped
14 ounces pasta ruffles, cooked, drained

Yield: 4 to 6 servings

- Combine the garlic and walnuts in a food processor container. Process until chopped.
- Add the spinach, cheese, olive oil, water, salt and basil.
- Process until well mixed, adding additional water if a thinner sauce is desired. Stir in the tomato.
- Spoon the sauce over the pasta, tossing to coat well.
- Serve hot.

Lazy Lasagna

15 ounces ricotta cheese

1 egg

2 tablespoons chopped parsley

1/2 teaspoon oregano

2 (16-ounce) jars spaghetti sauce

8 ounces uncooked lasagna noodles

16 ounces mozzarella cheese, shredded

2 tablespoons freshly grated Parmesan cheese

Yield: 6 to 8 servings

- Mix the ricotta cheese, egg, parsley and oregano in a bowl.
- Spread 1½ cups of the spaghetti sauce in a 9x13-inch baking pan.
- Layer the uncooked noodles and cheese mixture ½ at a time over the sauce.
- Top with the remaining sauce and mozzarella cheese.
- Sprinkle with the Parmesan cheese.
- Chill, covered, for 8 to 12 hours.
- Bake, uncovered, at 350 degrees for 50 minutes to 1 hour or until bubbly and heated through.
- Let stand for 15 minutes before serving.

Veggie Lasagna

The unique variety of cheeses gives this dish extra flavor.

10 lasagna noodles

2 (10-ounce) packages frozen chopped spinach

1/2 cup chopped onion

2 cups sliced fresh mushrooms

1 to 2 tablespoons vegetable oil

1 (15-ounce) can tomato sauce

1 (6-ounce) can tomato paste

1/2 teaspoon oregano

1 cup grated carrot

1 to 2 cloves of garlic, minced

1/4 teaspoon basil

2 cups cottage cheese

1 pound Monterey Jack cheese, shredded

1/4 cup grated Parmesan cheese

Yield: 6 to 8 servings

- Cook the noodles using the package directions; drain.
- Cook the spinach using the package directions; drain.
- Sauté the onion and mushrooms in the oil in a skillet.
- Stir in the tomato sauce, tomato paste, oregano, carrot, garlic, basil and spinach.
- Simmer until heated through.
- Layer the noodles, cottage cheese, spinach mixture, Monterey Jack cheese and Parmesan cheese 1/2 at a time in a greased 9x13-inch baking pan.
- Bake, covered, at 350 degrees for 30 minutes or until bubbly.

Fettuccini with Tomato Yogurt Sauce

1/4 cup olive oil

1 medium onion, chopped

1 1/2 tablespoons minced garlic

2 (28-ounce) cans stewed tomatoes

Salt and black pepper to taste

2 tablespoons fresh basil, or
   1 teaspoon dried oregano

1 tablespoon olive oil

6 to 8 slices bacon, chopped

1 cup yogurt

1 pound fettuccini, cooked, drained

1 teaspoon crushed red pepper

Grated Parmesan cheese to taste

Fresh basil to taste

Yield: 4 to 6 servings

- Heat 1/4 cup olive oil in a saucepan.
- Add the onion and garlic.
- Sauté until the vegetables are soft.
- Purée the sautéed vegetables and tomatoes in batches in a food processor; return the mixture to the saucepan.
- Add salt, black pepper and 2 tablespoons basil.
- Simmer over low heat for 45 minutes to 1 hour or until the sauce has thickened and the liquid is reduced, stirring frequently.
- Heat 1 tablespoon olive oil in a small skillet.
- Add the bacon.
- Cook over low heat until the bacon is softened and the fat has rendered; set aside without draining.
- Whisk the yogurt into 2 cups of the tomato sauce; reserve the remainder of the tomato sauce for another use.
- Toss the fettuccini with the undrained bacon and red pepper.
- Arrange the fettuccini on individual serving plates.
- Top with the tomato yogurt sauce.
- Sprinkle with the cheese and fresh basil to taste.

MIDNIGHT SNACKS

STAINED GLASS WINDOW IN DIMNENT CHAPEL AT HOPE COLLEGE

*Memories of graduations, weddings, and
concerts flooded my mind.*

Lois Lamb

Midnight Snacks

*Most requested recipe
from **Eet Smakelijk**

Michigan Apple Orchard Cake

3 cups flour
1 teaspoon salt
1 teaspoon baking soda
1 teaspoon cinnamon
3 eggs
1¹/₂ cups vegetable oil
2 cups sugar
2 teaspoons vanilla extract
3 cups chopped apples
1 cup chopped pecans
1 cup flaked coconut
¹/₂ cup margarine, softened
1 cup packed brown sugar
¹/₄ cup milk

Yield: 16 servings

- Sift the flour, salt, baking soda and cinnamon together.
- Beat the eggs, oil and sugar in a large mixer bowl.
- Add the flour mixture to the egg mixture; mix well.
- Stir in the vanilla, apples, pecans and coconut.
- Pour the batter into a greased and floured large bundt pan.
- Bake at 350 degrees for 45 minutes or until a wooden pick inserted near the center comes out clean.
- Cool in the pan on a wire rack for 1 to 2 minutes.
- Invert the cake onto a serving plate; cool slightly
- Mix the margarine, brown sugar and milk in a bowl until of spreading consistency.
- Spread the frosting over the top and side of the cake.

Chocolate Chip Cake

1 (2-layer) package yellow cake mix

1/2 cup vegetable oil

2 cups chocolate chips

1 cup sour cream

1 (4-ounce) package chocolate instant
  pudding mix

4 eggs

2 tablespoons rum

Yield: 16 servings

- Combine the cake mix, oil, chocolate chips, sour cream, pudding mix, eggs and rum in a large mixer bowl; mix for 7 minutes.
- Pour the batter into a nonstick bundt pan.
- Bake at 325 degrees for 55 minutes to 1 hour or until the top cracks and dries.

Chocolate Cinnamon Cake

*P*erfect for birthday celebrations.

3 cups flour

1/2 cup baking cocoa

2 teaspoons baking soda

1 1/2 teaspoons cinnamon

1 teaspoon salt

1 cup butter, softened

2 1/4 cups sugar

2 eggs

1 teaspoon vanilla extract

2 cups buttermilk

Yield: 12 servings

- Sift the flour, cocoa, baking soda, cinnamon and salt into a bowl.
- Cream the butter, sugar and eggs in a mixer bowl until light and fluffy. Beat in the vanilla.
- Add the flour mixture and the buttermilk alternately to the creamed mixture, beating well after each addition. Pour the batter into 2 greased and floured round cake pans.
- Bake at 350 degrees for 45 minutes.
- Cool in the pans for several minutes; remove to a wire rack to cool completely.
- Spread a rich chocolate frosting between the layers and over the top and side of the cake.

Mississippi Mud Cake

4 eggs

2 cups sugar

1½ cups flour

1 cup melted margarine

⅓ cup baking cocoa

1 cup chopped pecans

1 cup flaked coconut

1 (14-ounce) can marshmallow creme

½ cup margarine, softened

½ cup baking cocoa

½ cup evaporated milk

1 teaspoon vanilla extract

1 (16-ounce) package confectioners' sugar

1 cup chopped pecans

Yield: 15 servings

- Beat the eggs, sugar and flour lightly in a bowl.
- Add a mixture of the melted margarine and ⅓ cup cocoa.
- Stir in 1 cup pecans and 1 cup coconut.
- Pour the batter into a greased 9x13-inch cake pan.
- Bake at 350 degrees for 30 minutes.
- Spread the marshmallow creme over the hot cake.
- Combine ½ cup margarine and ½ cup cocoa in a mixer bowl.
- Beat in the evaporated milk, vanilla, confectioners' sugar and 1 cup pecans; mix until slightly thickened.
- Spread the confectioners' sugar mixture over the cooled cake.

Red Velvet Cake

A colorful way to make Valentine's Day extra sweet.

1½ cups sugar

½ cup shortening

2 eggs

2 ounces red food coloring

2 tablespoons baking cocoa

2½ cups flour

1 teaspoon salt

1 cup buttermilk

1 teaspoon vanilla extract

1 tablespoon vinegar

1 teaspoon baking soda

1⅓ cups milk

⅓ cup flour

2 cups confectioners' sugar

1 cup margarine, softened

½ teaspoon vanilla extract

½ teaspoon almond extract

Yield: 12 servings

- Cream the sugar and shortening in a mixer bowl until light and fluffy.
- Add the eggs 1 at a time, beating well after each addition. Beat in the food coloring and cocoa.
- Add the flour and salt alternately with the buttermilk, beating well after each addition.
- Beat in 1 teaspoon vanilla. Mix the vinegar and baking soda in a small glass and add immediately to the batter; mix well with a spoon. Pour the batter into 2 greased and floured round cake pans.
- Bake at 325 degrees for 30 to 45 minutes or until the layers test done.
- Cool the layers in the pans for several minutes; remove to a wire rack to cool completely.
- Add enough of the milk to the flour to make of paste consistency.
- Bring the remaining milk to a boil in a saucepan.
- Add the flour paste. Cook until the mixture is thickened, stirring constantly; cool completely.
- Beat the confectioners' sugar and margarine in a mixer bowl until light and thickened.
- Add the milk mixture; beat until the mixture is the consistency of whipped cream.
- Beat in ½ teaspoon vanilla and the almond flavoring.
- Spread the frosting between the layers and over the top and side of the cake.

Gooey Butter Cake

1 (16-ounce) package pound cake mix
½ cup melted butter
2 eggs
8 ounces cream cheese, softened
2 eggs
½ teaspoon vanilla extract
3½ cups confectioners' sugar
1 cup chopped pecans
½ cup confectioners' sugar

Yield: 15 servings

- Combine the cake mix, butter and 2 eggs in a mixer bowl, stirring until well blended; beat for 1 minute.
- Spread the batter in a greased 9x13-inch cake pan.
- Beat the cream cheese in a mixer bowl until light and fluffy. Beat in the 2 eggs and vanilla.
- Beat in the 3½ cups confectioners' sugar. Pour evenly over the batter in the pan. Sprinkle with the pecans.
- Bake at 350 degrees for 35 to 45 minutes or until the cake pulls away from the sides of the pan.
- Cool in the pan for 20 minutes. Sprinkle with ½ cup confectioners' sugar.

Mexican Wedding Cake

2 cups flour
1 cup each sugar and brown sugar
1 (16-ounce) can crushed pineapple
1 cup chopped pecans
2 teaspoons each vanilla extract and baking soda
2 eggs
11 ounces cream cheese, softened
¾ cup margarine, softened
1 cup sugar
1 teaspoon vanilla extract

Yield: 15 servings

- Combine the flour, 1 cup sugar, brown sugar, undrained pineapple, pecans, 2 teaspoons vanilla, baking soda and eggs in a bowl; mix well.
- Pour the batter into a 9x13-inch nonstick cake pan.
- Bake at 350 degrees for 25 to 30 minutes or until the cake tests done.
- Combine the cream cheese, margarine, 1 cup sugar and 1 teaspoon vanilla in a mixer bowl; beat well.
- Spread the frosting over the cooled cake.

PEACH KUCHEN*

2 cups flour
1/4 teaspoon baking powder
1/2 teaspoon salt
1 cup sugar
1/2 cup butter
12 fresh or frozen peach halves
1 teaspoon cinnamon
2 egg yolks, lightly beaten
1 cup cream or half-and-half

Yield: 6 servings

- Sift the flour, baking powder, salt and 2 tablespoons of the sugar into a large bowl.
- Cut in the butter until crumbly.
- Pat the mixture over the bottom and halfway up the sides of a greased 8x8-inch baking dish.
- Arrange the peaches over the pastry; sprinkle the peaches with a mixture of the cinnamon and remaining sugar.
- Bake at 400 degrees for 15 minutes.
- Mix the egg yolks and cream in a bowl and pour over the peaches.
- Bake for 30 minutes longer.
- Serve warm.

Pumpkin Nut Roll

3/4 cup flour

1 teaspoon baking powder

2 teaspoons cinnamon

1 teaspoon ginger

1/2 teaspoon nutmeg

1/2 teaspoon salt

3 eggs

1 cup sugar

1 teaspoon lemon juice

2/3 cup pumpkin

1 cup chopped pecans

1 cup confectioners' sugar

6 ounces cream cheese, softened

1/4 cup butter, softened

1/2 teaspoon vanilla extract

Yield: 12 servings

- Line a jelly roll pan with foil placed shiny side down; grease and flour the foil.
- Sift the flour, baking powder, cinnamon, ginger, nutmeg and salt together.
- Beat the eggs at high speed in a mixer bowl for 5 minutes.
- Add the sugar, lemon juice and pumpkin; beat well.
- Add the flour mixture gradually, beating well after each addition.
- Spread the mixture in the prepared pan.
- Top with the pecans.
- Bake at 375 degrees for 15 minutes.
- Turn the bread onto a towel, pecan side down; do not use a terry cloth towel.
- Remove the foil carefully.
- Roll up the bread and towel together, beginning at the small end.
- Chill the bread thoroughly.
- Mix the confectioners' sugar, cream cheese, butter and vanilla in a bowl until of spreading consistency.
- Unroll the bread and spread the cream cheese mixture over the side without the pecans.
- Reroll the bread without the towel.
- Chill until serving time.
- Cut the roll into 1-inch slices.

Applesauce Pie

*This pie has a wonderful, custard-like consistency and is a nice alternative to pumpkin at Thanksgiving.

2 eggs
1 cup sugar
1/2 cup melted butter
1 cup applesauce
2 tablespoons flour
1/2 teaspoon vanilla extract
2 tablespoons lemon juice
3 tablespoons quick-cooking tapioca
1 unbaked (9-inch) pie shell

Yield: 8 servings

- Combine the eggs, sugar, melted butter, applesauce, flour, vanilla, lemon juice and tapioca in a bowl; mix well.
- Pour the mixture into the pie shell.
- Bake at 350 degrees for 45 to 50 minutes or until the center is set.
- *Note:* Omit the lemon juice if the applesauce is tart.

DUTCH APPLE PIE*

5 to 6 tart apples, sliced

³/₄ cup sugar

1 teaspoon cinnamon

1 unbaked (9-inch) pie shell

²/₃ cup flour

¹/₂ cup packed brown sugar

¹/₃ cup margarine

Yield: 6 servings

- Mix the apples, sugar and cinnamon in a bowl.
- Spoon the mixture into the pie shell.
- Mix the flour, brown sugar and margarine in a bowl until crumbly. Sprinkle the mixture over the apples.
- Bake·at 425 degrees for 15 minutes.
- Reduce the oven temperature to 375 degrees.
- Bake for 35 minutes longer.

CRANBERRY PIE

This pie tastes best when made with real butter and prepared a day in advance.

2 cups fresh whole cranberries

¹/₂ cup sugar

¹/₂ cup chopped English walnuts

2 eggs

1 cup sugar

1 cup flour

¹/₂ cup melted butter

¹/₄ cup melted shortening

Yield: 8 servings

- Spread the cranberries in a greased 10-inch pie plate.
- Sprinkle a mixture of ¹/₂ cup sugar and walnuts over the cranberries.
- Beat the eggs in a mixer bowl.
- Add the 1 cup sugar gradually, beating until well mixed.
- Add the flour, butter and shortening; beat well.
- Pour the mixture over the cranberries.
- Bake at 325 degrees for 1 hour or until the crust is golden brown.
- Serve warm or cold with vanilla ice cream.

Granny's Graham Cracker Pie

16 graham crackers, finely crushed

1 teaspoon flour

¼ cup shortening

¼ cup melted butter

½ cup sugar

1½ tablespoons cinnamon

¼ teaspoon salt

3 egg yolks

½ cup sugar

2 tablespoons cornstarch

2 cups milk

¼ teaspoon salt

1 teaspoon vanilla extract

3 egg whites

3 tablespoons sugar

Yield: 8 servings

- Mix the graham cracker crumbs, flour, shortening, butter, ½ cup sugar, cinnamon and ¼ teaspoon salt in a bowl.
- Reserve a small amount of the mixture for the topping; press the remaining mixture into a pie plate.
- Mix the egg yolks, ½ cup sugar, cornstarch, milk and ¼ teaspoon salt in a medium saucepan.
- Cook over low heat until the custard coats the spoon, stirring constantly.
- Stir in the vanilla.
- Pour over the prepared layer.
- Beat the egg whites with 3 tablespoons sugar in a mixer bowl until stiff peaks form.
- Spread over the custard.
- Sprinkle with the reserved crumb mixture.
- Bake at 325 degrees for 15 minutes.

Frozen Mocha Pie

1¹/₄ cups chocolate wafer crumbs

¹/₄ cup sugar

¹/₄ cup margarine

8 ounces cream cheese, softened

1 (14-ounce) can sweetened condensed milk

²/₃ cup chocolate fudge syrup

2 tablespoons instant coffee

1 teaspoon hot water

1 cup whipping cream, whipped

Yield: 8 servings

- Combine the wafer crumbs, sugar and margarine in a bowl.
- Press the mixture into a 9-inch springform pan or a pie plate.
- Beat the cream cheese in a mixer bowl until light and fluffy.
- Blend in the condensed milk and chocolate syrup.
- Dissolve the coffee powder in the hot water and stir into the chocolate mixture.
- Fold in the whipped cream.
- Pour the mixture into the prepared crust.
- Freeze until firm.

Auburn Restaurant's Peanut Butter Sin

1 cup chocolate wafer crumbs

1/2 cup finely chopped pecans

6 tablespoons melted unsalted butter

1 1/4 cups creamy peanut butter

8 ounces cream cheese, softened

1/2 cup confectioners' sugar

2 tablespoons melted unsalted butter

1 1/4 cups chilled whipping cream

1/2 cup confectioners' sugar

1 tablespoon vanilla extract

1/2 cup whipping cream

4 ounces semisweet chocolate, finely chopped

Yield: 8 servings

- Mix the wafer crumbs, pecans and 6 tablespoons butter in a 9-inch round pie plate; press the mixture over the bottom and side of the pie plate. Freeze until needed.

- Beat the peanut butter, cream cheese, 1/2 cup confectioners' sugar and 2 tablespoons butter in a large mixer bowl.

- Beat 1 1/4 cups whipping cream with 1/2 cup confectioners' sugar and vanilla in a medium mixer bowl until soft peaks form.

- Stir 1/4 of the whipped cream mixture into the peanut butter mixture.

- Fold in the remaining whipped cream mixture.

- Spoon the mixture into the prepared crust, reserving a small amount for garnish. Chill until firm.

- Bring 1/2 cup whipping cream to a boil in a small heavy saucepan; reduce the heat to low.

- Add the chocolate.

- Cook until the chocolate is melted and the mixture is smooth, stirring constantly.

- Cool the glaze slightly.

- Pour the glaze over the filling, tilting the pie plate to cover the filling completely.

- Garnish with rosettes of filling.

- Chill for 1 hour or longer.

Pumpkin Pecan Pie

1 cup packed brown sugar

¹/₂ teaspoon cinnamon

¹/₄ teaspoon salt

1 cup canned pumpkin

3 eggs, beaten

¹/₂ cup dark corn syrup

1 teaspoon vanilla extract

1 unbaked (9-inch) pie shell

³/₄ cup coarsely chopped pecans

¹/₄ cup pecan halves

¹/₂ cup packed brown sugar

¹/₂ teaspoon cinnamon

¹/₈ teaspoon nutmeg

³/₄ cup whipping cream

¹/₂ teaspoon vanilla extract

Yield: 8 servings

- Mix 1 cup brown sugar, ¹/₂ teaspoon cinnamon and salt in a large bowl.
- Stir in the pumpkin, eggs, corn syrup and 1 teaspoon vanilla; mix well.
- Spoon the mixture into the pie shell.
- Sprinkle with the chopped pecans and arrange the pecan halves over the top.
- Bake at 350 degrees for 40 minutes or until a knife inserted near the center comes out clean.
- Cool the pie to room temperature.
- Combine ¹/₂ cup brown sugar, ¹/₂ teaspoon cinnamon and nutmeg in a mixer bowl.
- Stir in the whipping cream and ¹/₂ teaspoon vanilla.
- Whip the mixture until stiff peaks form.
- Chill for 1 hour.
- Spread the whipped cream mixture over the pie.

Southern Pecan Pie

3 eggs, beaten
³⁄₄ cup dark corn syrup
³⁄₄ cup packed brown sugar
¹⁄₄ teaspoon salt
2 teaspoons vanilla extract
3 tablespoons melted butter
1¹⁄₄ cups pecan halves
1 unbaked (9-inch) pie shell

Yield: 8 servings
- Blend the eggs and corn syrup in a bowl.
- Stir in the brown sugar, salt and vanilla.
- Fold in the butter and pecans.
- Pour the mixture into the pie shell.
- Bake at 375 degrees for 45 minutes.

Dutch Strawberry Pie*
(Aardbeien Pie)

1 quart strawberries
¹⁄₂ cup confectioners' sugar
1 cup water
¹⁄₂ to ³⁄₄ cup sugar
2 tablespoons cornstarch
1 baked (9-inch) pie shell

Yield: 6 to 8 servings
- Combine the strawberries and confectioners' sugar in a large bowl; mix well.
- Remove 1 cup of the smaller berries from the mixture and crush.
- Combine the crushed strawberries with the water in a saucepan. Cook for 2 minutes.
- Stir in a mixture of the sugar and cornstarch.
- Cook until the mixture is clear and thickened.
- Fill the pie shell with the whole strawberry mixture.
- Pour the cooked mixture over the top.
- Chill until serving time.

Apple Cheesecake

Easy to prepare and tastes fabulous, this is a nice fall dessert.

½ cup melted butter or margarine

⅓ cup sugar

1 cup flour

¼ teaspoon vanilla extract

8 ounces cream cheese, softened

¼ cup sugar

1 egg

½ teaspoon vanilla extract

3 cups thinly sliced apples

⅓ cup sugar

1 teaspoon cinnamon

Sliced almonds to taste (optional)

Yield: 16 servings

- Mix the butter, ⅓ cup sugar, flour and ¼ teaspoon vanilla in a bowl.
- Press the mixture over the bottom and 1 inch up the side of a 9-inch springform pan.
- Mix the cream cheese, ¼ cup sugar, egg and ½ teaspoon vanilla in a bowl.
- Pour the mixture over the prepared layer.
- Toss the apples with ⅓ cup sugar and cinnamon in a bowl.
- Spoon the apple mixture over the cream cheese mixture.
- Sprinkle with the almonds.
- Bake at 450 degrees for 10 minutes.
- Reduce the oven temperature to 400 degrees.
- Bake for 25 minutes longer.
- Cool in the pan.

Sandpiper Pumpkin Amaretto Cheesecake

Bring some of the elegance of the Sandpiper Restaurant into your home.

1½ cups graham cracker crumbs

2 tablespoons sugar

1 teaspoon cinnamon

6 tablespoons melted butter

¼ cup sugar

¼ cup packed brown sugar

16 ounces cream cheese, softened

3 eggs

2 tablespoons flour

½ teaspoon cinnamon

1 tablespoon vanilla extract

1 cup pumpkin

¼ cup amaretto

Yield: 12 servings

- Mix the graham cracker crumbs, 2 tablespoons sugar and 1 teaspoon cinnamon in a bowl.
- Stir in the butter.
- Press the mixture over the bottom and halfway up the side of a 9-inch springform pan.
- Cream ¼ cup sugar, brown sugar and cream cheese in a mixer bowl until light and fluffy.
- Add the eggs 1 at a time, beating well after each addition.
- Stir in a mixture of the flour and ½ teaspoon cinnamon.
- Beat in the vanilla, pumpkin and amaretto.
- Pour the mixture into the prepared pan.
- Press heavy-duty foil tightly over the bottom and side of the pan to prevent leakage.
- Set the pan into a larger shallow pan of hot water.
- Bake in the water bath at 375 degrees for 20 minutes.
- Reduce the oven temperature to 275 degrees.
- Bake for 1½ to 2 hours longer or until a wooden pick inserted near the center comes out clean.

Nancy Potter's Pumpkin Cheesecake

One-of-the-best shares one of her secrets.

1½ cups gingersnap crumbs

½ cup sugar

½ cup melted butter

24 ounces cream cheese, softened

3 cups packed brown sugar

6 eggs

1 cup sour cream

2 cups canned pumpkin

2 teaspoons vanilla extract

2 teaspoons cinnamon

1 teaspoon nutmeg

1 teaspoon ginger

1 teaspoon cloves

Yield: 16 servings

- Mix the cookie crumbs, sugar and butter in a bowl.
- Press the mixture over the bottom and side of a 9-inch springform pan sprayed with nonstick cooking spray.
- Combine the cream cheese and brown sugar in a mixer bowl and mix well.
- Add the eggs and sour cream, mixing well at low speed.
- Stir in the pumpkin, vanilla, cinnamon, nutmeg, ginger and cloves.
- Mix at low speed until completely blended; mixing at high speeds will cause air to enter the mixture and the cheesecake will crack during baking.
- Pour into the prepared pan.
- Press heavy-duty foil tightly over the bottom and side of the pan to prevent leakage.
- Set the pan into a larger shallow pan of hot water.
- Bake in the water bath at 325 degrees for 2 hours.
- Turn off the oven; let the cheesecake stand in the closed oven for 2 hours.
- Chill for 6 hours.
- Dip the knife into hot water before cutting each slice so that the cuts will be clean.

Butterscotch Apple Pecan Cobbler

2¹/2 pounds apples, peeled, chopped
2 cups butterscotch chips
¹/4 cup packed brown sugar
¹/4 cup flour
¹/2 teaspoon cinnamon
¹/2 cup flour
¹/4 cup packed brown sugar
¹/4 cup butter
1 cup chopped pecans
³/4 cup quick-cooking or rolled oats

Yield: 10 to 12 servings

- Arrange the apples in a 9x13-inch baking pan.
- Sprinkle a mixture of the butterscotch chips, ¹/4 cup brown sugar, ¹/4 cup flour and cinnamon over the apples.
- Bake at 375 degrees for 20 minutes.
- Combine the remaining ¹/2 cup flour and ¹/4 cup brown sugar in a bowl.
- Cut in the butter until crumbly.
- Stir in the pecans and oats.
- Sprinkle the oat mixture over the baked layer.
- Bake for 30 to 40 minutes longer or until the apples are tender.
- Cool slightly.
- Serve with ice cream or whipped cream.

Field Trip Apple Crunch

Dozens of apple orchards dot the greater Holland area, and local schoolchildren visit these orchards each fall.

1 cup quick-cooking oats

5 cups flour

1 cup packed brown sugar

¹/₂ cup butter

3 cups chopped apples

1 tablespoon flour

1 teaspoon cinnamon, or to taste

¹/₈ teaspoon salt

1 tablespoon water

5 cups sugar

Yield: 8 to 10 servings

- Mix the oats, 5 cups flour and brown sugar in a large bowl.
- Cut in the butter until crumbly.
- Mix the apples, 1 tablespoon flour, cinnamon, salt, water and sugar in a medium bowl.
- Layer the brown sugar mixture and the apple mixture ¹/₂ at a time in a nonstick 9x9-inch baking pan.
- Bake at 350 degrees for 45 minutes or until the apples are tender.

Blueberry Crisp

4 cups blueberries

1 tablespoon lemon juice

1 cup sugar

2¹/₂ tablespoons cornstarch

¹/₂ teaspoon each cinnamon and nutmeg

¹/₂ teaspoon grated lemon peel

¹/₃ (2-layer) package yellow cake mix

6 to 8 tablespoons melted butter

¹/₂ cup chopped pecans (optional)

Yield: 6 servings

- Toss the blueberries gently with the lemon juice in a medium casserole. Add the sugar, cornstarch, cinnamon, nutmeg and lemon peel, mixing gently.
- Sprinkle with the cake mix and drizzle with the melted butter. Top with the pecans.
- Bake at 350 degrees for 50 to 55 minutes or until golden brown.
- Serve warm or cold with ice cream.

BLUEBERRY TRIFLE

This tastes best with fresh Michigan blueberries.

1 (6-ounce) package French vanilla
   instant pudding mix
12 ounces whipped topping
18 to 24 ladyfingers
⅓ cup dry or cream sherry
2 cups fresh or frozen blueberries
⅓ cup raspberry preserves

Yield: 8 to 10 servings

- Prepare the pudding mix using slightly less milk than the package directions specify.
- Fold in the whipped topping.
- Separate the ladyfingers into halves.
- Line a 2-quart glass serving bowl with some of the ladyfingers, placing flat side to bowl.
- Drizzle most of the sherry over the ladyfingers.
- Sprinkle ⅓ of the berries over the ladyfingers; cover the berries with half the pudding mixture.
- Layer the remaining ladyfingers over the pudding; sprinkle with the remaining sherry.
- Spread the ladyfingers with the preserves.
- Sprinkle half the remaining blueberries over the preserves.
- Top with the remaining pudding mixture and blueberries.
- Chill, covered with plastic wrap, for several hours to overnight.
- Garnish with whipped cream.
- May prepare the dessert in individual dishes and may add layers of peaches.

Triple Berry Cobbler

1¼ cups flour

1 tablespoon baking powder

¾ teaspoon salt

3 tablespoons sugar

¾ cup plus 2 tablespoons milk

1 egg

3 tablespoons melted butter

½ teaspoon vanilla extract

1½ pints blackberries

3 pints blueberries

1½ pints raspberries

¾ cup sugar

½ teaspoon cinnamon

¼ teaspoon ginger

1 teaspoon flour

½ teaspoon vanilla extract

Yield: 8 to 10 servings

- Combine the 1¼ cups flour, baking powder, salt and 3 tablespoons sugar in a mixer bowl; mix at low speed.
- Add the milk and beat at high speed until smooth.
- Beat in the egg, butter and ½ teaspoon vanilla at low speed.
- Cover the bowl with plastic wrap and set aside.
- Mix the berries, ¾ cup sugar, cinnamon, ginger, 1 teaspoon flour and ½ teaspoon vanilla in a bowl.
- Pour the berry mixture into a buttered 10-inch baking dish.
- Pour the batter over the berries to within 1 inch of the side.
- Bake at 400 degrees for 35 to 45 minutes or until brown.
- Serve warm or at room temperature.
- Serve plain or topped with vanilla ice cream or whipped cream.
- May substitute frozen berries if fresh are not in season.

Clearbrook's Dried Cherry and Hazelnut Bread Pudding

Candice Finchem, pastry chef at Clearbrook Restaurant, contributed this rich delight.

4 cups cinnamon roll, croissant or
French bread cubes

1/3 cup dried cherries

1/3 cup toasted hazelnuts

4 eggs

2 1/4 cups half-and-half

3/4 cup sugar

1 tablespoon vanilla extract

1/2 cup unsalted butter

1 cup sugar

2 egg yolks

1/4 cup water

1/4 cup dark rum

Yield: 8 to 10 servings

- Arrange half the bread in an 8x8-inch baking pan sprayed with nonstick baking spray.
- Sprinkle with the cherries and half the hazelnuts.
- Cover with the remaining bread and hazelnuts.
- Beat the eggs in a bowl.
- Add the half-and-half, 3/4 cup sugar and vanilla, beating well.
- Pour the egg mixture over the bread, pressing down to evenly distribute the mixture.
- Bake at 350 degrees until a knife inserted near the center comes out clean.
- Combine the butter, 1 cup sugar, egg yolks and water in a saucepan, mixing with a wire whisk.
- Cook over medium heat until the sugar is dissolved and just until the mixture bubbles; remove from the heat.
- Stir in the rum and cool slightly.
- Serve with the warm bread pudding.
- May substitute other nuts for the hazelnuts and other liquor for the rum.

Till Midnight's Midnight Torte

1 pound bittersweet chocolate
1 cup unsalted butter
6 eggs

Yield: 8 to 10 servings

- Melt the chocolate and butter in a double boiler over simmering water.
- Break the eggs into a bowl.
- Whisk the eggs over the same simmering water until warm to the touch.
- Pour the eggs into a mixer bowl and beat at high speed for 6 minutes or until foamy and tripled in volume.
- Fold the eggs ½ at a time into the chocolate mixture, folding gently to maintain the volume.
- Pour the mixture into a 9-inch springform pan.
- Press heavy-duty foil tightly over bottom and side of the pan to prevent leakage.
- Place the pan in a larger pan filled with hot water.
- Bake at 425 degrees for 15 minutes.
- Remove the torte from the oven gently; the torte will not be set.
- Let stand at room temperature for 1 hour.
- Chill for 4 hours.
- Place the springform pan in a pan of hot water for 30 seconds; unmold the torte onto a serving plate.
- Garnish with whipped cream, fresh berries and chocolate curls.

Turtle Torte

Very rich.

2 cups roasted pecans
¹/₃ cup sugar
¹/₄ cup melted butter
1¹/₂ cups whipping cream
2 cups semisweet chocolate chips
³/₄ cup crushed pecans
1 jar caramel topping, warmed

Yield: 12 to 16 servings

- Chop the roasted pecans with the sugar in a food processor.
- Add the butter and mix well.
- Press the mixture into a springform pan.
- Bake at 350 degrees for 20 to 25 minutes or until golden brown.
- Combine the whipping cream and chocolate chips in a saucepan; bring to a simmer.
- Cook over low heat until the chocolate is melted and the mixture is smooth, whisking constantly.
- Cool to lukewarm and pour into the cooled crust.
- Chill for 30 minutes or longer.
- Sprinkle the crushed pecans around the edge of the torte.
- Loosen and remove the side of the pan.
- Pour the caramel sauce slowly over the torte in a checkerboard pattern.
- Chill until serving time.
- Garnish the sides with whole pecans.

Rice Chex Ice Cream

2½ cups crushed Rice Chex
1 cup packed brown sugar
1 cup split cashews
½ cup melted butter
1 cup flaked coconut
½ gallon vanilla ice cream

Yield: 10 to 12 servings

- Combine the cereal, brown sugar, cashews, butter and coconut in a bowl.
- Spread half the cereal mixture, the ice cream and the remaining cereal mixture in a 9x10-inch dish.

Pumpkin Crumble

A delicious yet simple way to please a holiday crowd.

1 (16-ounce) can pumpkin
1 cup sugar
1 teaspoon cinnamon
⅛ teaspoon nutmeg, or to taste
2 eggs, beaten
1 (8-ounce) can evaporated milk
1 (2-layer) package yellow cake mix
2 cups chopped walnuts
½ cup melted butter

Yield: 15 servings

- Mix the pumpkin, sugar, cinnamon and nutmeg in a bowl.
- Add the eggs, mixing well.
- Blend in the evaporated milk.
- Pour the mixture into a greased 9x13-inch baking pan.
- Sprinkle with the cake mix and walnuts.
- Pour the butter evenly over the walnuts.
- Bake at 350 degrees for 45 to 55 minutes or until golden brown; do not allow the walnuts to burn.

$\mathcal{C}$ONTRIBUTORS

Jackie Anderson
Brenda Athey
Deborah Bailey
Susan Bartolomei
Judy Batts
Helen Bickel
Jennifer Bieri
Ronald Binkowski
Cheryl Clarke
Rachelle Coleman
Linda Dahm
Barb Davidson
Barb DePree
Gina Dobbin
Kirsen Doolittle
Pat Eldean
Barb Ellis
Judy Faber
Holly Fabiano
Candice Finchem
Luke Finchem
Susan Formsma
Kim Franken
Margaret Franken
Kathy Frieling
Shirley Frieling
Mary Claire Fu
Tom Gebben
Kristine Gezon
Heidi Gilcrest
Sally Haveman
Josie Heidenreich
Jill Henderson

Annie Hoffman
Deb Hoksbergen
Holly Hudson-Hatt
Julie Huisingh
Lillian Huisingh
Amanda Hutchinson
Susan Hutchinson
Suzanne Immink
Laura Ipema
Melynda Jabaay
Emily Jarzembowski
Judith Jarzembowski
Karri Jasperse
Cathy Jelsema
Candy Jeltema
Jim Jeltema
Marion Jones
Lisa Keller
Myra Keuning
Laura Klakulak
Mary-Jo Kooiker
Sue Kraai
Lois Lamb
Lisa Lindemulder
Michele Lonergan
Lisa Luckey
Helen Lynam
Diane Main
Kristi Maki
Tom Nienhuis
Tina Nyland
Nancy Padnos
Donald Pellegrini

Michelle Pellegrini
Cindy Peterson
Nancy Potter
Jaymi Ratzlaff
Natalie Rawlings
Nancy Rebhan
Wendy Rebhan
Betsy Rhein
Debra Rollans
Leesa Schram
Kathy Skrivan
Penne Smith
Jan Spoelhof
Joel Spykerman
Sandy Stehle
Deb Sterken
Stephanie Strand
Mike Struk
Antoinette Swaney
Spring Sweeny
Mark Tanis
Butch Ter Haar
Mary Beth Theisen
Deborah Troutman
Beth Tyler
Kristin Vande Bunte
Todd Van Wieren
Larry Wagenaar
Jill Walcott
Lynn White
Wendy Willoughby
Janet Winter
Sheryl Wright

We also wish to extend our gratitude to everyone whose efforts in the past and present have made—and those whose efforts in the future will continue to make—"Dawn to Dusk" a success. To the many contributors to "Eet Smakelijk," especially those whose recipes appear in this book and whose past efforts inspired us, we also say thank you.

INDEX

235

ORDER FORM

Holland Junior Welfare League
P.O. Box 1633
Holland, Michigan 49422

BOOK TITLE	QUANTITY	PRICE PER BOOK*	TOTAL
Eet Smakelijk		$17.50	$
Dawn to Dusk		22.50	
Dutch Treat**		35.00	
		Grand Total	$

Name _____

Address _____

City _____ State _____ Zip _____

*Price includes shipping and handling charge. **Includes one copy each of Eet Smakelijk and Dawn to Dusk.

The proceeds from the sales of these cookbooks will be disbursed to qualifying applicants who share in our passion for the welfare of our community's youth.

Holland Junior Welfare League
P.O. Box 1633
Holland, Michigan 49422

BOOK TITLE	QUANTITY	PRICE PER BOOK*	TOTAL
Eet Smakelijk		$17.50	$
Dawn to Dusk		22.50	
Dutch Treat**		35.00	
		Grand Total	$

Name _____

Address _____

City _____ State _____ Zip _____

*Price includes shipping and handling charge. **Includes one copy each of Eet Smakelijk and Dawn to Dusk.

The proceeds from the sales of these cookbooks will be disbursed to qualifying applicants who share in our passion for the welfare of our community's youth.

Photocopied and handwritten orders also accepted.